Blast off into a universe of discovery with the **"Amazing and Super Fun Facts Quiz Book About Space Mysteries and Wonders"**! This interactive book is perfect for curious kids aged 8+, filled with intriguing quizzes and fascinating facts about space mysteries, deep space exploration, space phenomena, pioneers in space, and water in space.

What's Inside?

- **Space Mysteries**: Venture into the unknown and explore the greatest mysteries of the cosmos. From dark matter and black holes to the enigmatic forces that shape our universe, challenge your knowledge and unravel the secrets of space.

- **Deep Space Exploration**: Discover the incredible missions and technologies that allow us to explore the farthest reaches of space. Learn about groundbreaking spacecraft, pioneering missions, and the future of interstellar travel.

- **Space Phenomena**: Delve into the awe-inspiring phenomena of the universe. From mesmerizing auroras and meteor showers to the birth of stars and galaxies, explore the wonders that make space so fascinating.

- **Pioneers in Space**: Celebrate the brave men and women who have made significant contributions to space exploration. Learn about their journeys, achievements, and the legacy they leave for future generations.

- **Water in Space**: Investigate the presence and significance of water beyond our planet. Understand how the discovery of water on other celestial bodies impacts the search for life and future space missions.

Why You'll Love This Book

- **Interactive Learning**: Each section starts with an engaging quiz to test your knowledge, followed by detailed answers and fun facts that make learning exciting and memorable.

- **Educational Fun**: Perfect for kids who love to learn while having fun. This book combines education and entertainment, making it a great tool for parents and teachers alike.

- **Perfect Gift**: Ideal for birthdays, holidays, or any occasion. Encourage a love of learning and exploration in your child with this delightful book.

Best Ways to Use This Book

- **Family Quiz Nights:** Bring the whole family together for a fun and educational quiz night. Challenge each other with fascinating questions and learn new facts together!

- **Road Trip Entertainment:** Keep your child entertained on long car rides with engaging quizzes and captivating stories about the wonders of space.

- **Classroom Fun:** Teachers can use this book as a fun educational tool to spark students' interest in astronomy and space science.

- **Friend Challenges:** Kids can quiz their friends and see who knows the most about space mysteries, deep space exploration, phenomena, pioneers, and water in space.

Discover, Learn, and Be Amazed!

With the **"Amazing and Super Fun Facts Quiz Book About Space,"** your child will not only learn about the wonders of the universe but will also develop critical thinking skills and a lifelong love for knowledge. Perfect for road trips, rainy days, or family quiz nights, this book promises hours of educational fun.

Legal Notice

This book is intended for educational and entertainment purposes only. The information provided herein is accurate and true to the best of the author's knowledge, but there may be errors, omissions, or inaccuracies. The author and publisher disclaim any liability in connection with the use of this book.

TABLE OF CONTENTS

Dark Matter's Dance: A Cosmic Chance

Quiz Question

1. What is dark matter made of?

Options

A. Ordinary atoms
B. Dark atoms
C. Unknown particles
D. Light particles

C. Unknown particles

Dark matter is composed of unknown particles that don't interact with light, making it invisible. Scientists can't see it directly but know it exists because of its gravitational effects on galaxies and stars. It's one of the universe's greatest mysteries!

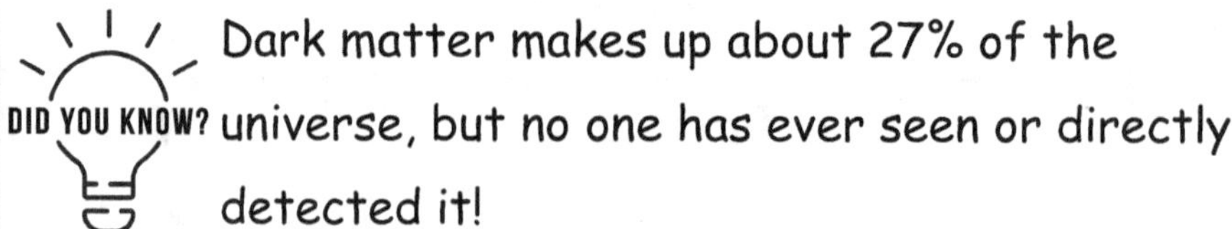

DID YOU KNOW? Dark matter makes up about 27% of the universe, but no one has ever seen or directly detected it!

Dark Matter's Dance: A Cosmic Chance

Quiz Question

2. How do scientists detect dark matter?

Options

A. By light

B. By sound

C. Through gravity

D. Using mirrors

C. Through gravity

Even though dark matter is invisible, scientists detect it by observing its gravitational pull on visible objects like stars and galaxies. This helps them understand how much dark matter is out there.

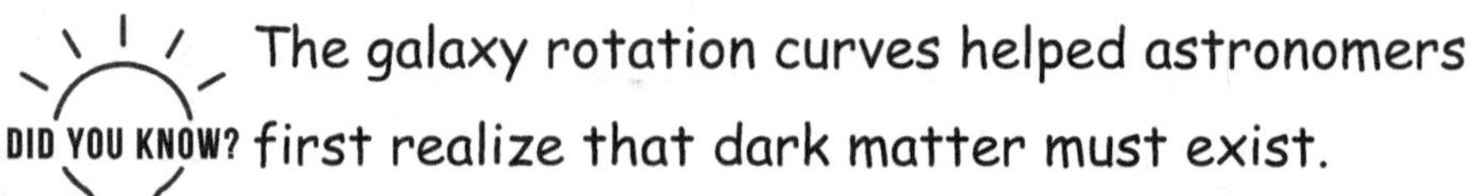

DID YOU KNOW? The galaxy rotation curves helped astronomers first realize that dark matter must exist.

Dark Matter's Dance: A Cosmic Chance

Quiz Question

3. Where is dark matter mostly found?

Options

A. In stars
B. In black holes
C. In galaxies
D. In the ocean

C. In galaxies

Dark matter is mostly found in and around galaxies. It forms a "halo" around them, helping to hold the galaxies together with its gravity.

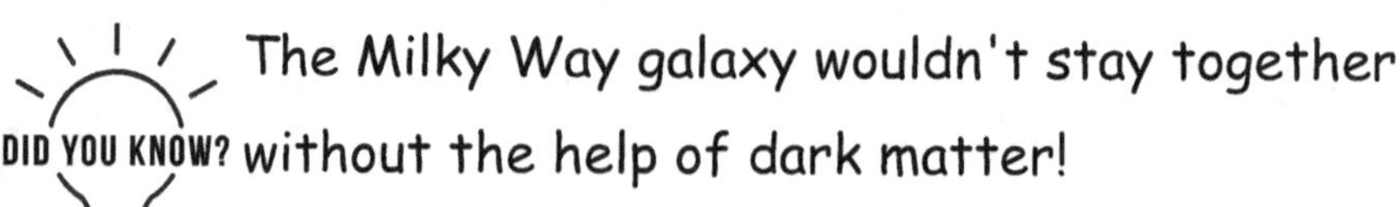

DID YOU KNOW? The Milky Way galaxy wouldn't stay together without the help of dark matter!

Quiz Question

4. Why is dark matter important?

Options

A. It helps plants grow

B. It shapes galaxies

C. It produces light

D. It causes earthquakes

B. It shapes galaxies

Dark matter's gravitational pull shapes the structure and formation of galaxies, influencing the universe's overall architecture. Without it, galaxies might not have formed in the way they have.

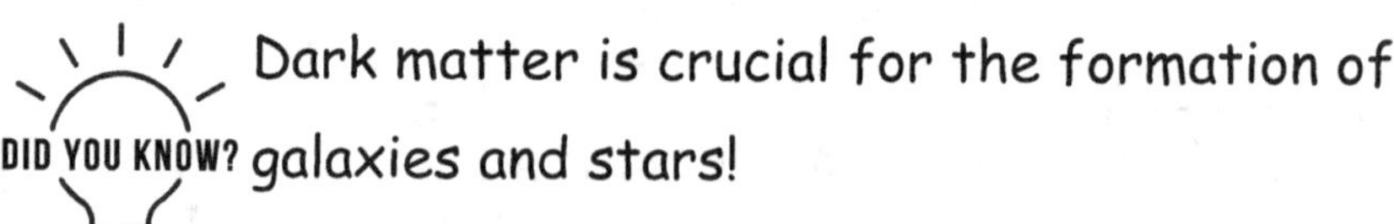

Dark matter is crucial for the formation of galaxies and stars!

Dark Matter's Dance: A Cosmic Chance

Quiz Question

5. When was the concept of dark matter first proposed?

Options

A. 1800s
B. 1930s
C. 1950s
D. 1970s

B. 1930s

The concept of dark matter was first proposed in the 1930s by Swiss astronomer Fritz Zwicky. He noticed that galaxies were moving faster than expected and suggested that an invisible mass must be present to hold them together.

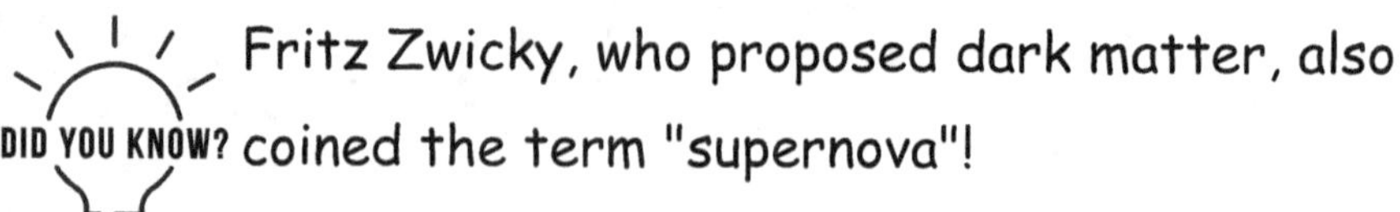

Fritz Zwicky, who proposed dark matter, also DID YOU KNOW? coined the term "supernova"!

Energy's Whirl: A Galactic Swirl

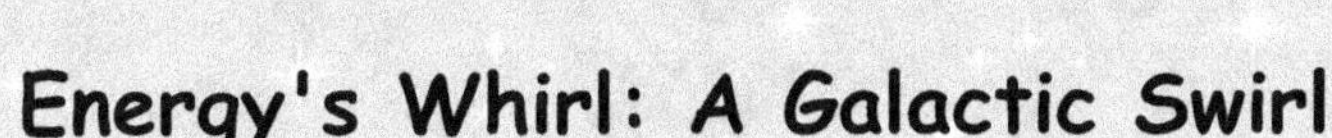

Quiz Question

1. What is dark energy?

Options

| A. An explosion |
| B. A mysterious force |
| C. A type of star |
| D. Earth's core |

B. A mysterious force

Dark energy is a mysterious force causing the universe to expand at an accelerating rate. Scientists don't fully understand it, but it's believed to make up about 68% of the universe.

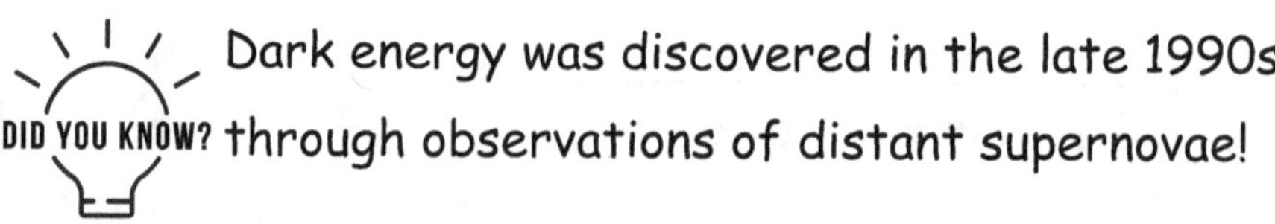

DID YOU KNOW? Dark energy was discovered in the late 1990s through observations of distant supernovae!

Quiz Question

2. How does dark energy affect the universe?

Options

A. Slows it down
B. Stops it
C. Speeds up expansion
D. Shrinks it

C. Speeds up expansion

Dark energy speeds up the universe's expansion, making galaxies move away from each other faster over time. This is opposite to the effect of gravity.

The universe's expansion was slower in the past before dark energy became dominant!

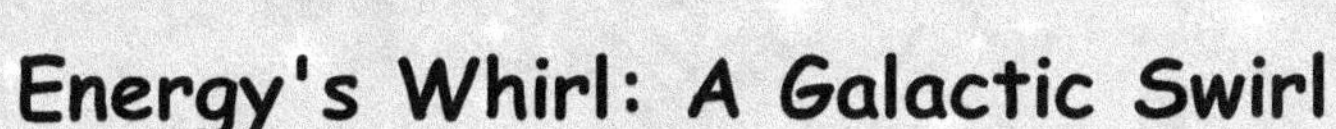

Quiz Question

3. What tool do scientists use to study dark energy?

Options

A. Telescopes

B. Stethoscopes

C. Microscopes

D. Thermometers

A. Telescopes

Scientists use telescopes to observe distant galaxies and supernovae to study dark energy. These observations help them understand how the universe's expansion rate changes over time.

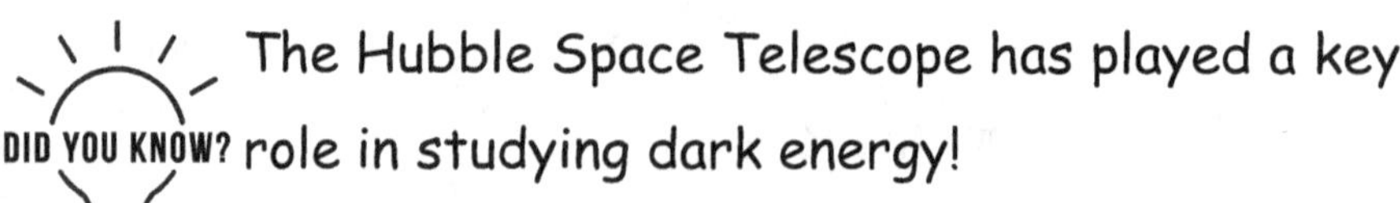

The Hubble Space Telescope has played a key role in studying dark energy!

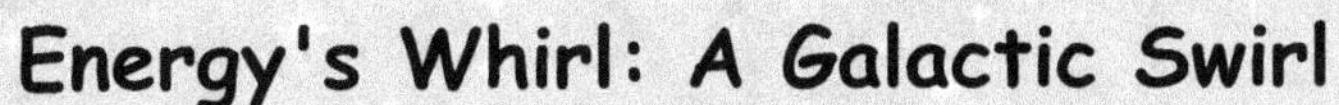

Energy's Whirl: A Galactic Swirl

Quiz Question

4. Who first discovered the accelerating expansion of the universe?

Options

A. Albert Einstein
B. Edwin Hubble
C. Henrietta Leavitt
D. Two separate teams

D. Two separate teams

Two separate teams, one led by Saul Perlmutter and the other by Brian Schmidt and Adam Riess, discovered the universe's accelerating expansion in the late 1990s.

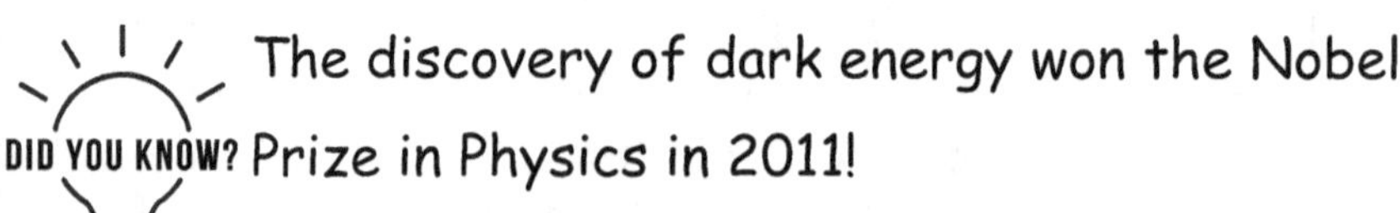

The discovery of dark energy won the Nobel Prize in Physics in 2011!

5. How much of the universe is made up of dark energy?

Options

A. 0.05
B. 0.27
C. 0.5
D. 0.68

D. 68%

Dark energy comprises about 68% of the universe. This dominant force is still a mystery but plays a crucial role in the universe's fate.

• • • • • • • • • • • • • • •

DID YOU KNOW? Together, dark matter and dark energy make up about 95% of the universe!

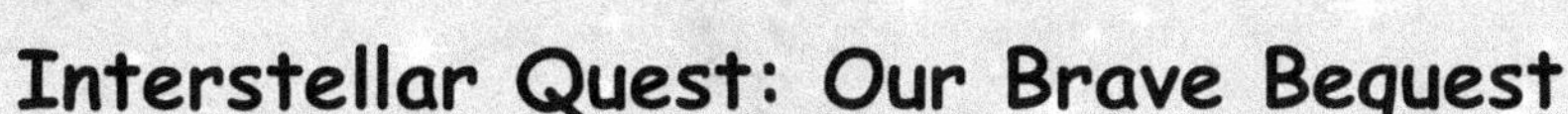

Quiz Question

1. What is an interstellar mission?

Options

A. A trip to the Moon

B. Exploring other stars

C. Building new planets

D. Observing the Sun

B. Exploring other stars

Interstellar missions involve traveling to other stars and exploring their surroundings. This is a challenging and exciting goal for future space exploration.

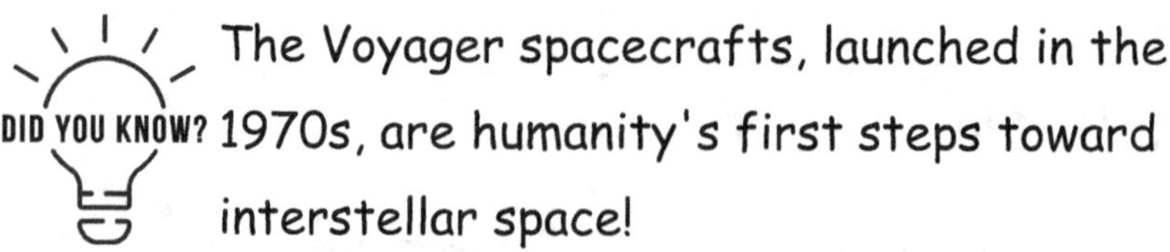

DID YOU KNOW? The Voyager spacecrafts, launched in the 1970s, are humanity's first steps toward interstellar space!

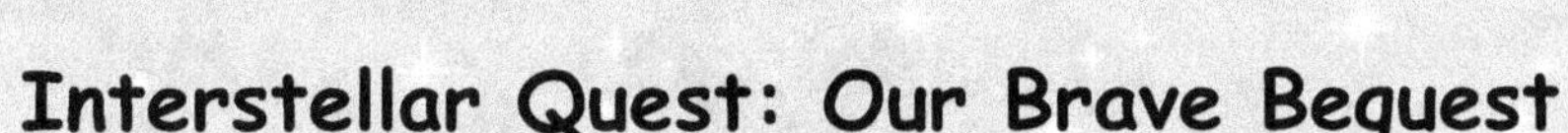

Interstellar Quest: Our Brave Bequest

Quiz Question

2. Which spacecraft is currently on an interstellar mission?

Options

A. Apollo 11
B. Voyager 1
C. ISS
D. Hubble

B. Voyager 1

Voyager 1, launched in 1977, is currently on an interstellar mission, traveling beyond our solar system into interstellar space.

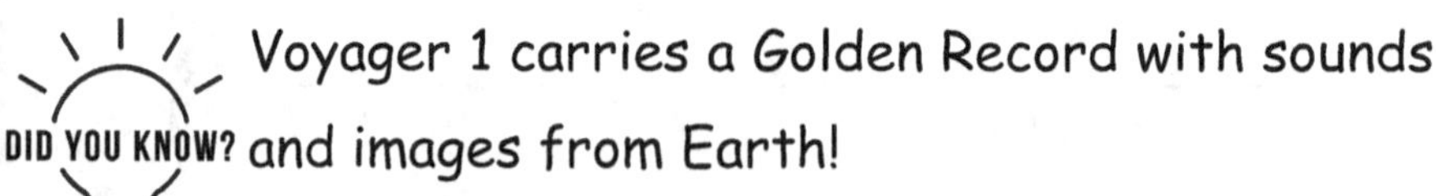

Voyager 1 carries a Golden Record with sounds

DID YOU KNOW? and images from Earth!

Interstellar Quest: Our Brave Bequest

Quiz Question

3. How long does it take to reach another star?

Options

A. 1 year

B. 10 years

C. 100 years

D. Thousands of years

D. Thousands of years

Traveling to even the nearest star, Proxima Centauri, would take thousands of years with current spacecraft technology. This highlights the challenges of interstellar travel.

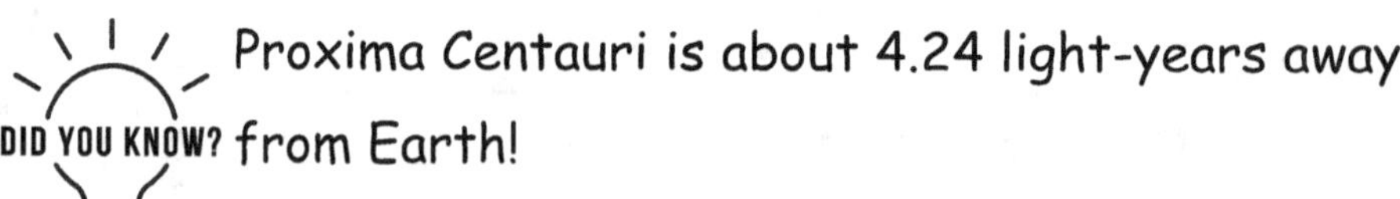

Proxima Centauri is about 4.24 light-years away from Earth!

Quiz Question

4. What is the goal of interstellar missions?

Options

A. To find new life

B. To mine asteroids

C. To build space stations

D. To find aliens

A. To find new life

One of the main goals of interstellar missions is to search for new life forms and understand the possibilities of life beyond Earth.

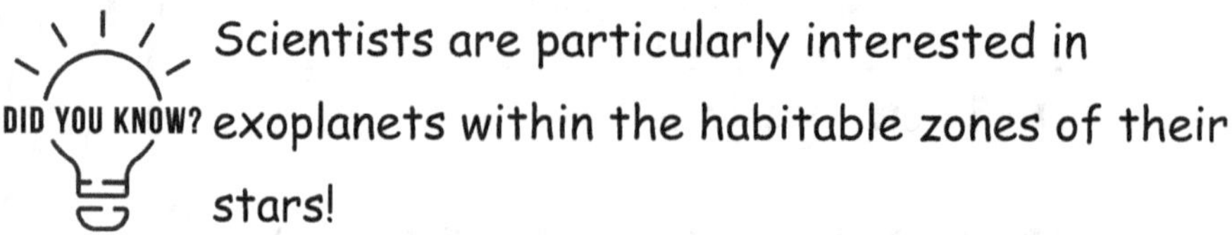

DID YOU KNOW? Scientists are particularly interested in exoplanets within the habitable zones of their stars!

Interstellar Quest: Our Brave Bequest

Quiz Question

5. What technology might be used for interstellar missions?

Options

A. Wind sails

B. Solar sails

C. Rockets

D. Submarines

B. Solar sails

Solar sails could potentially be used for interstellar missions. They use sunlight for propulsion, allowing spacecraft to travel vast distances without traditional fuel.

• • • • • • • • • • • • • • • • • • • •

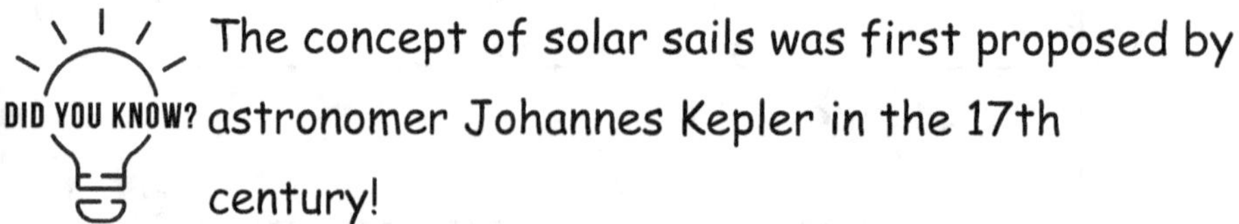

The concept of solar sails was first proposed by astronomer Johannes Kepler in the 17th century!

DID YOU KNOW?

Exoplanet Dreams: Beyond Moonbeams

Quiz Question

1. What is an exoplanet?

Options

A. A moon
B. An asteroid
C. A planet outside our solar system
D. A comet

C. A planet outside our solar system

Exoplanets are planets that orbit stars outside our solar system. They come in many sizes and types, from gas giants to rocky worlds.

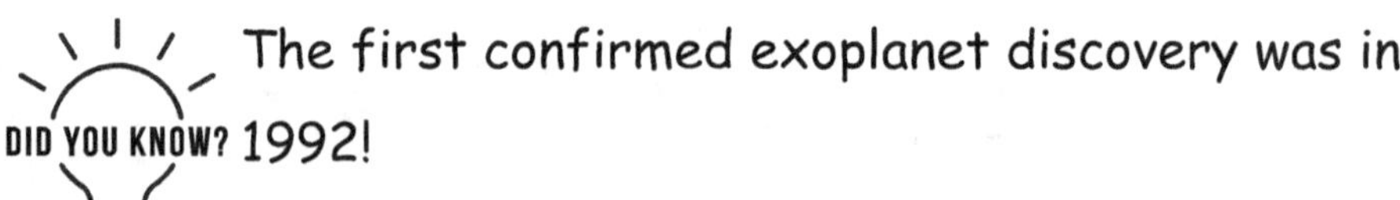

The first confirmed exoplanet discovery was in 1992!

DID YOU KNOW?

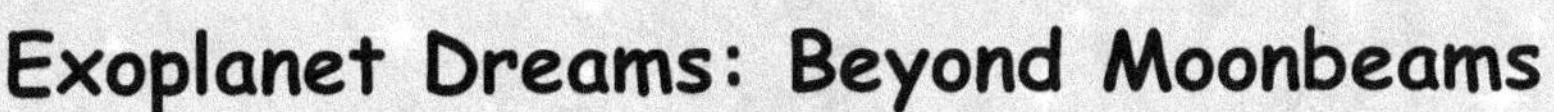

Exoplanet Dreams: Beyond Moonbeams

Quiz Question

2. How do scientists find exoplanets?

Options

A. By seeing them

B. By their shadows

C. By hearing them

D. By feeling them

B. By their shadows

Scientists often find exoplanets by observing the tiny dimming of a star's light as a planet passes in front of it, creating a shadow. This method is called the transit method.

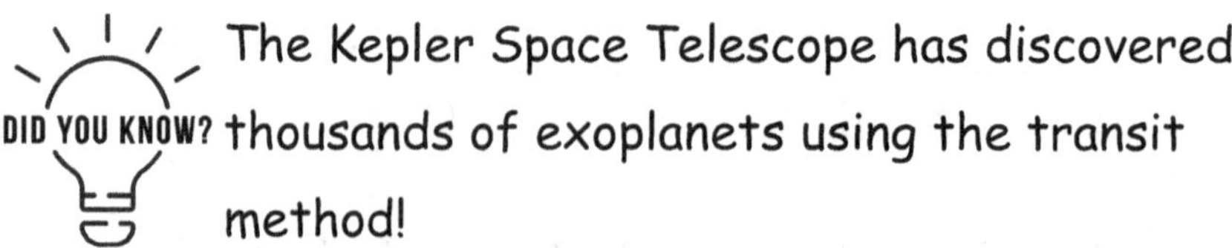

DID YOU KNOW? The Kepler Space Telescope has discovered thousands of exoplanets using the transit method!

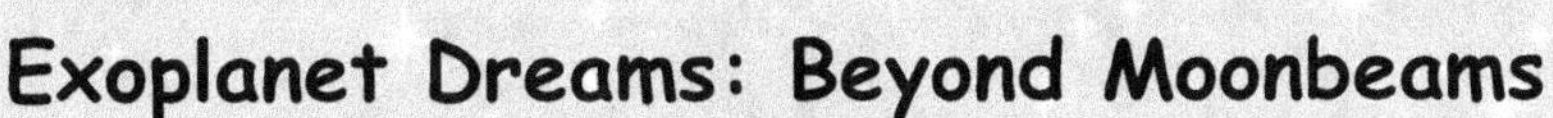

Quiz Question

3. What is the habitable zone?

Options

| A. The Sun's core |
| B. Earth's atmosphere |
| C. Area around a star where life could exist |
| D. A galaxy's center |

C. Area around a star where life could exist

The habitable zone, or "Goldilocks zone," is the area around a star where conditions might be just right for liquid water and potentially life.

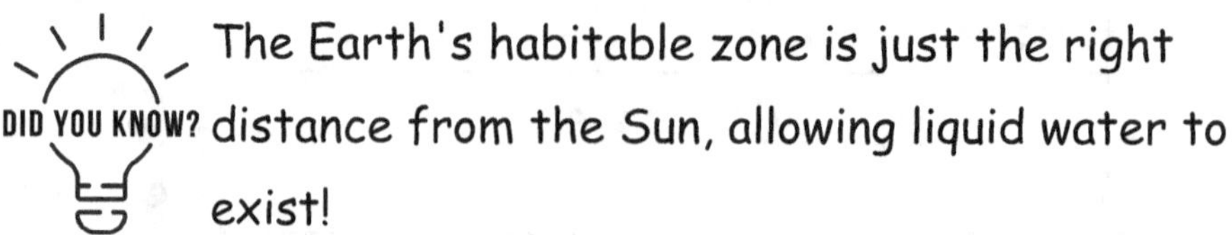

The Earth's habitable zone is just the right distance from the Sun, allowing liquid water to exist!

Quiz Question

4. Which exoplanet is most Earth-like?

Options

A. Jupiter

B. Proxima b

C. Neptune

D. Mars

B. Proxima b

Proxima b is an exoplanet orbiting the star Proxima Centauri. It's located in the habitable zone and is similar in size to Earth, making it a prime candidate for potential life.

· · · · · · · · · · · · · · · ·

DID YOU KNOW? Proxima b is the closest known exoplanet to Earth, about 4.24 light-years away!

Exoplanet Dreams: Beyond Moonbeams

Quiz Question

5. Why are exoplanets important?

Options

A. They produce energy

B. They hold keys to alien life

C. They are made of gold

D. They control tides

B. They hold keys to alien life

Exoplanets are important because they may hold clues to the existence of alien life. Studying them helps scientists understand the diversity of planets and the potential for life in the universe.

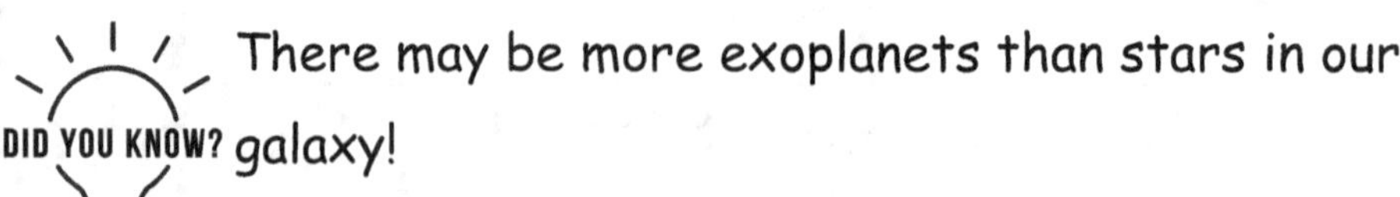

There may be more exoplanets than stars in our

DID YOU KNOW? galaxy!

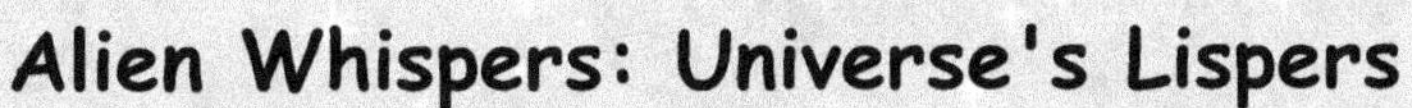

Quiz Question

1. What is the search for alien life called?

Options

A. Astronautics

B. SETI

C. Astrology

D. Aeronautics

B. SETI

The search for alien life is called SETI, which stands for the Search for Extraterrestrial Intelligence. Scientists use radio telescopes to listen for signals from alien civilizations.

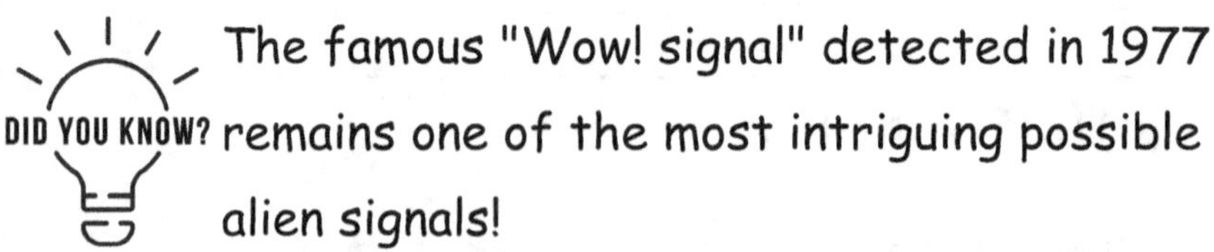

DID YOU KNOW? The famous "Wow! signal" detected in 1977 remains one of the most intriguing possible alien signals!

Quiz Question

2. What is a possible sign of alien life?

Options

A. Radio signals

B. Volcanoes

C. Mountains

D. Oceans

A. Radio signals

Scientists believe that detecting radio signals from space could be a sign of alien life. These signals might come from advanced civilizations trying to communicate.

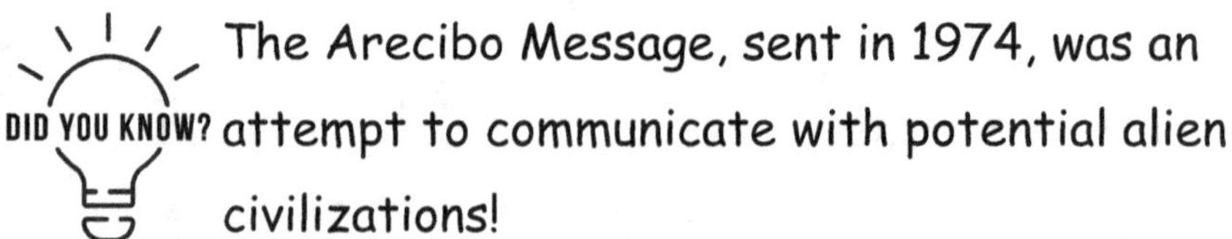

DID YOU KNOW? The Arecibo Message, sent in 1974, was an attempt to communicate with potential alien civilizations!

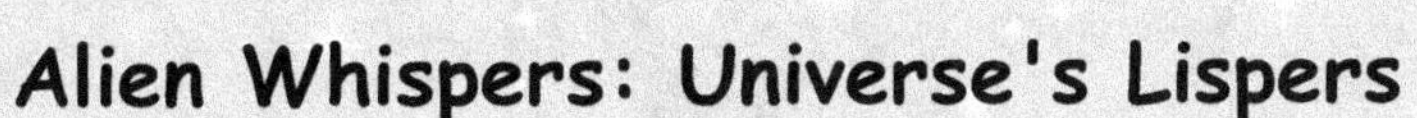

Quiz Question

3. What is the Drake Equation?

Options

A. A math puzzle

B. A recipe

C. A way to estimate alien civilizations

D. A star map

C. A way to estimate alien civilizations

The Drake Equation is a formula used to estimate the number of advanced alien civilizations in our galaxy. It takes into account factors like star formation rates and the likelihood of life.

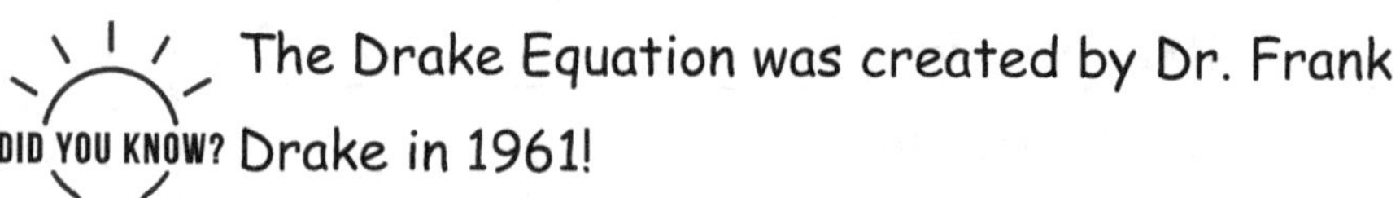

The Drake Equation was created by Dr. Frank Drake in 1961!

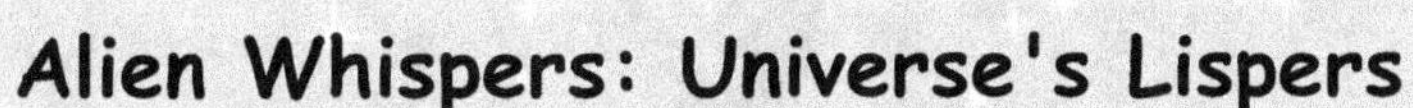

Quiz Question

4. Where might aliens live?

Options

A. On the Moon

B. In black holes

C. On exoplanets

D. In the sun

C. On exoplanets

Aliens might live on exoplanets, especially those in the habitable zones of their stars. These planets could have conditions suitable for life.

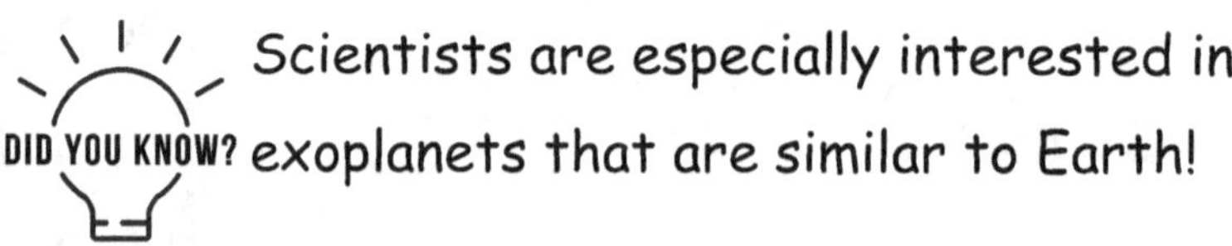

Scientists are especially interested in exoplanets that are similar to Earth!

Quiz Question

5. What is an alien megastructure?

Options

A. A spaceship

B. A star

C. A comet

D. A massive artificial structure

D. A massive artificial structure

An alien megastructure is a hypothetical massive artificial structure built by an advanced civilization, possibly to harness energy from a star.

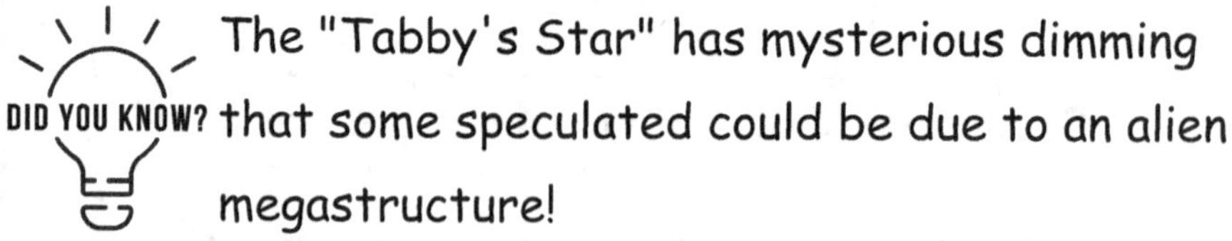

· · · · · · · · · · · · · · ·

DID YOU KNOW? The "Tabby's Star" has mysterious dimming that some speculated could be due to an alien megastructure!

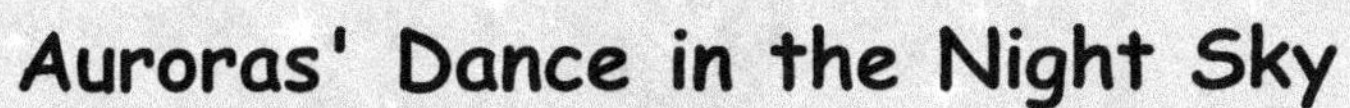

Auroras' Dance in the Night Sky

Quiz Question

1. What causes the beautiful colors in an aurora?

Options

A. Sun's heat
B. Earth's rotation
C. Solar wind particles colliding with atmosphere
D. Moonlight reflection

C. Solar wind particles colliding with atmosphere

Auroras are caused by the collision of solar wind particles with the Earth's atmosphere. When these charged particles collide with gases like oxygen and nitrogen, they emit light in various colors, creating breathtaking displays known as auroras. The colors depend on the type of gas and the altitude: green is common from oxygen at lower altitudes, while red and violet can appear from nitrogen higher up.

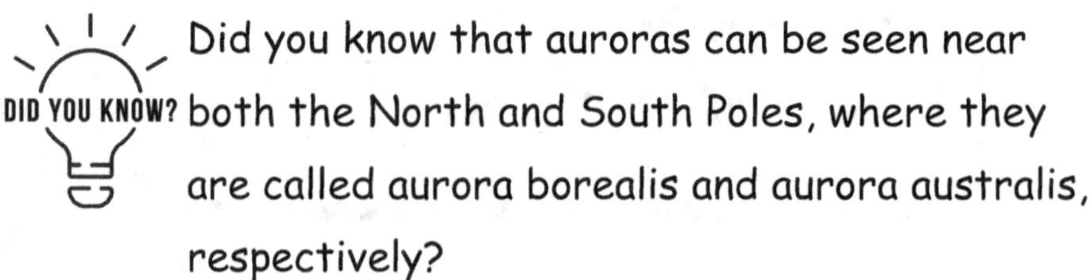

• • • • • • • • • • • • • • • • •

DID YOU KNOW? Did you know that auroras can be seen near both the North and South Poles, where they are called aurora borealis and aurora australis, respectively?

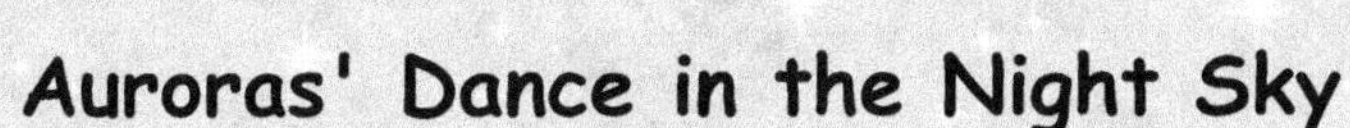

Quiz Question

2. Where are auroras most commonly seen?

Options

A. Equator
B. Poles
C. Tropics
D. Deserts

B. Poles

Auroras are most commonly seen near the polar regions because that's where Earth's magnetic field directs the solar wind particles. The North Pole has aurora borealis (Northern Lights), while the South Pole has aurora australis (Southern Lights). The closer you are to these poles, the more likely you are to witness this natural wonder.

• • • • • • • • • • • • • • • • • •

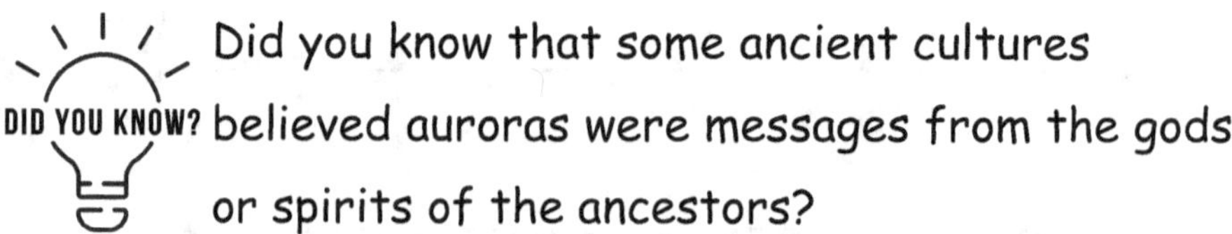

DID YOU KNOW? Did you know that some ancient cultures believed auroras were messages from the gods or spirits of the ancestors?

Auroras' Dance in the Night Sky

Quiz Question

3. What is another name for the Northern Lights?

Options

A. Aurora australis

B. Aurora equinox

C. Aurora borealis

D. Aurora noctis

C. Aurora borealis

The Northern Lights are scientifically known as aurora borealis. This name was coined by the astronomer Galileo Galilei, who combined the Roman goddess of dawn, Aurora, with the Greek word for the north wind, Boreas. The northern sky lights up with shimmering colors, creating a magical experience for all who see it.

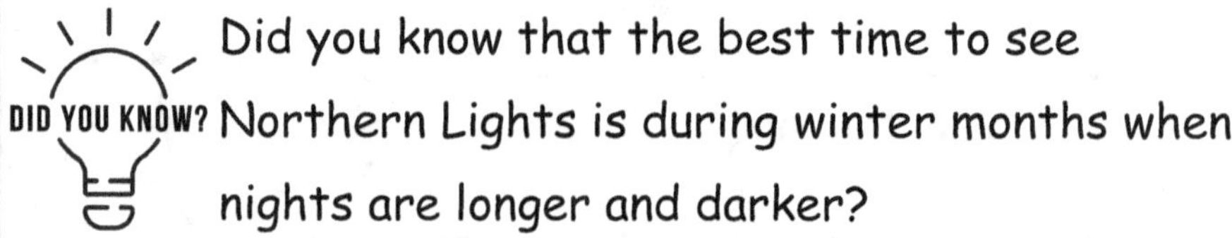

DID YOU KNOW? Did you know that the best time to see Northern Lights is during winter months when nights are longer and darker?

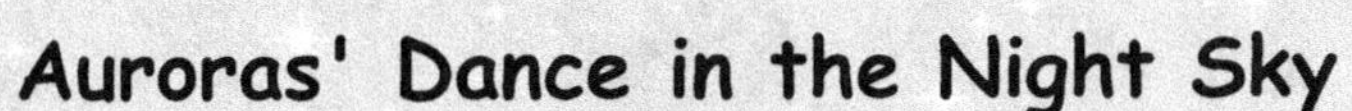

Quiz Question

4. Which gas in the atmosphere is responsible for green auroras?

Options

A. Helium
B. Oxygen
C. Carbon dioxide
D. Nitrogen

B. Oxygen

The green color in auroras is caused by oxygen molecules at lower altitudes, typically around 100 kilometers above the Earth. When these molecules are struck by charged solar particles, they emit a brilliant green light. The specific wavelength of light emitted corresponds to the green part of the visible spectrum.

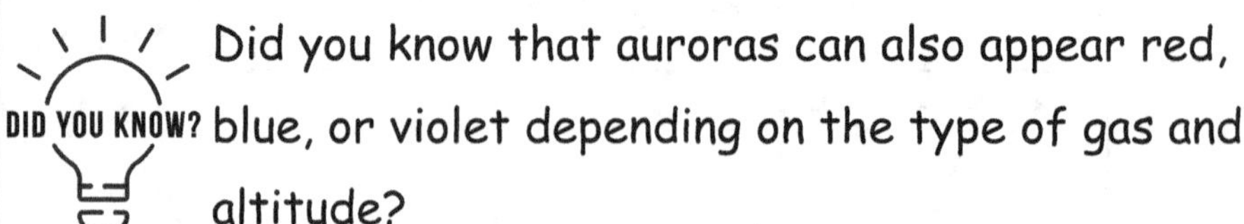

Did you know that auroras can also appear red, blue, or violet depending on the type of gas and altitude?

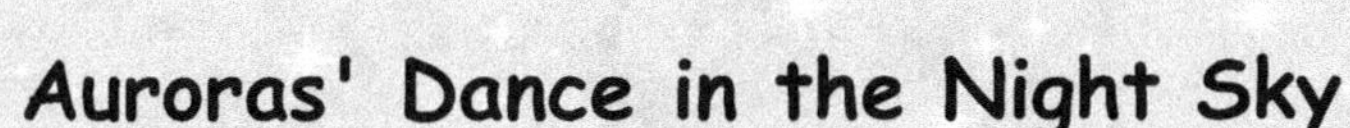

Auroras' Dance in the Night Sky

Quiz Question

5. What phenomenon creates the shape and movement of auroras?

Options

A. Ocean currents

B. Earth's magnetic field

C. Moon's gravity

D. Earth's spin

B. Earth's magnetic field

The shape and movement of auroras are influenced by Earth's magnetic field. The magnetic field lines direct the solar wind particles towards the poles, creating the curtains and arcs of light that move and dance across the sky. The interaction between these magnetic fields and solar particles creates the stunning, ever-changing displays.

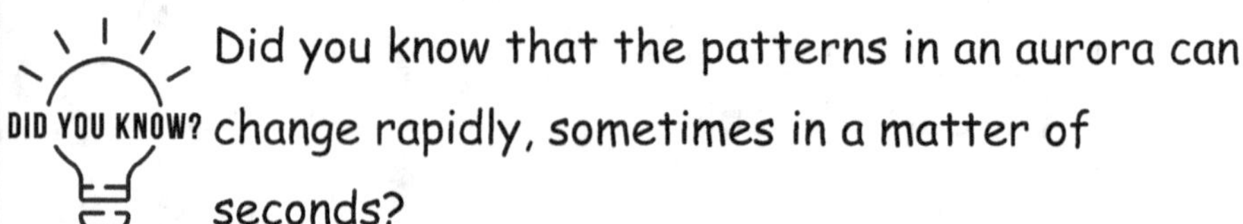

DID YOU KNOW? Did you know that the patterns in an aurora can change rapidly, sometimes in a matter of seconds?

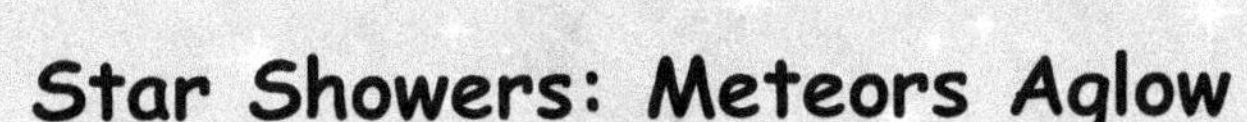

Star Showers: Meteors Aglow

Quiz Question

1. What causes a meteor shower?

Options

A. The Moon
B. Earth's gravity
C. Comets or asteroids
D. Sunlight

C. Comets or asteroids

Meteor showers occur when Earth passes through the debris left by a comet or asteroid. As these tiny particles enter Earth's atmosphere, they burn up due to friction, creating bright streaks of light in the sky known as meteors. These events can be predicted and often happen at the same time each year.

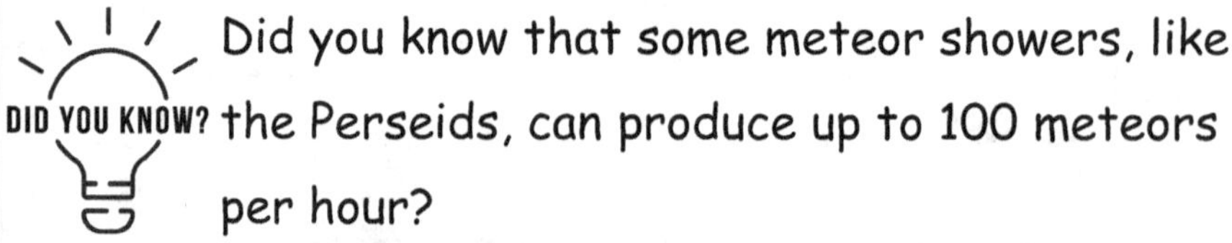

DID YOU KNOW? Did you know that some meteor showers, like the Perseids, can produce up to 100 meteors per hour?

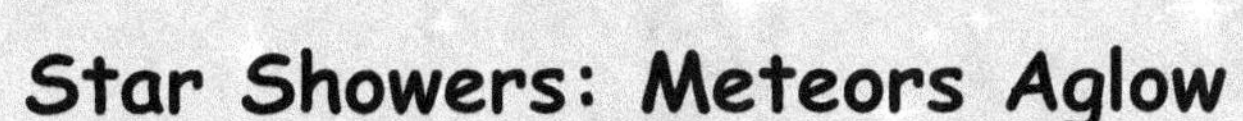

Quiz Question

2. What is another name for a meteor?

Options

A. Comet
B. Asteroid
C. Shooting star
D. Supernova

C. Shooting star

A meteor is often called a "shooting star" because of the bright streak of light it creates as it burns up in Earth's atmosphere. Despite the name, meteors are not actually stars but small particles from space that ignite due to friction.

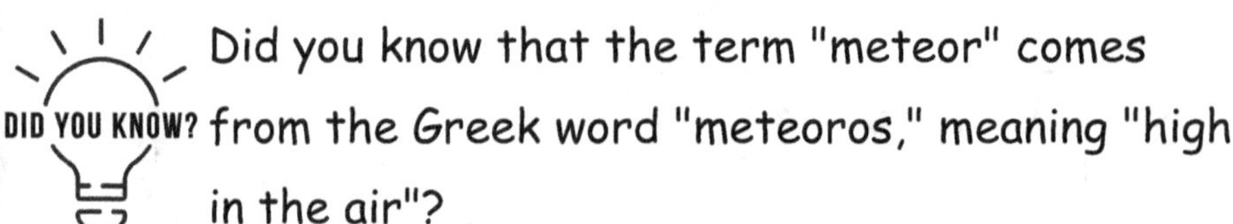

DID YOU KNOW? Did you know that the term "meteor" comes from the Greek word "meteoros," meaning "high in the air"?

Quiz Question

3. When is the Perseid meteor shower typically visible?

Options

A. January

B. April

C. August

D. December

C. August

The Perseid meteor shower is one of the most famous and is best visible in August. It is named after the constellation Perseus, from which the meteors appear to radiate. This annual event is a result of Earth passing through the debris left by the Swift-Tuttle comet.

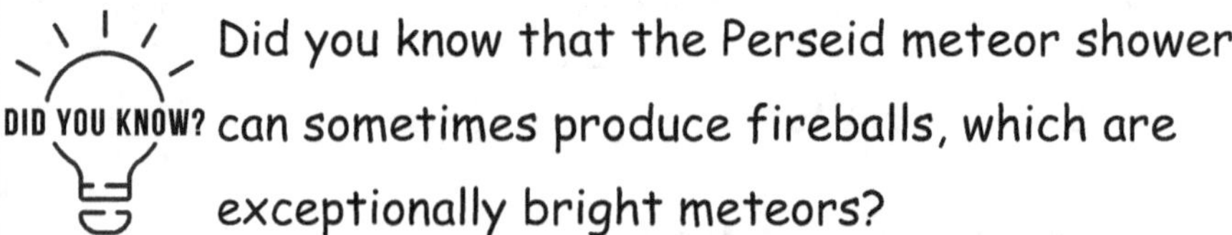

• • • • • • • • • • • • • • • • •

DID YOU KNOW? Did you know that the Perseid meteor shower can sometimes produce fireballs, which are exceptionally bright meteors?

Quiz Question

4. What is the term for a meteor that reaches Earth's surface?

Options

A. Meteorite
B. Meteoroid
C. Asteroid
D. Comet

A. Meteorite

When a meteor manages to pass through Earth's atmosphere and reaches the ground, it is called a meteorite. These space rocks can provide scientists with valuable information about the early solar system.

• • • • • • • • • • • • • • •

DID YOU KNOW? Did you know that the largest meteorite found on Earth, the Hoba meteorite in Namibia, weighs over 60 tons?

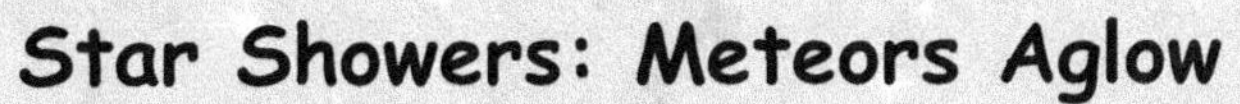

Quiz Question

5. What causes the different colors in meteors?

Options

A. Type of telescope

B. Speed of Earth's rotation

C. Composition of the meteor

D. Distance from the Sun

C. Composition of the meteor

The different colors in meteors are caused by the various elements they contain. For example, sodium produces a yellow color, iron creates a yellow-green hue, and magnesium results in a blue-white light. When these elements vaporize upon entering Earth's atmosphere, they emit specific colors.

DID YOU KNOW? Did you know that meteors can appear in a range of colors, from red and orange to green and blue?

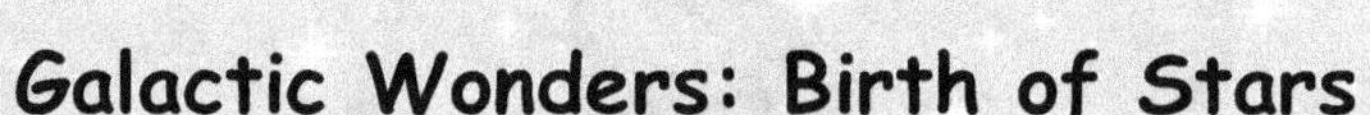

Quiz Question

1, Where do stars form?

Options

A. Black holes
B. Nebulae
C. Planets
D. Asteroids

B. Nebulae

Stars form in nebulae, which are vast clouds of gas and dust in space. These regions are often referred to as "stellar nurseries" because they provide the perfect conditions for star formation. Gravity pulls the gas and dust together, eventually igniting nuclear fusion, which marks the birth of a new star.

• • • • • • • • • • • • • • • • •

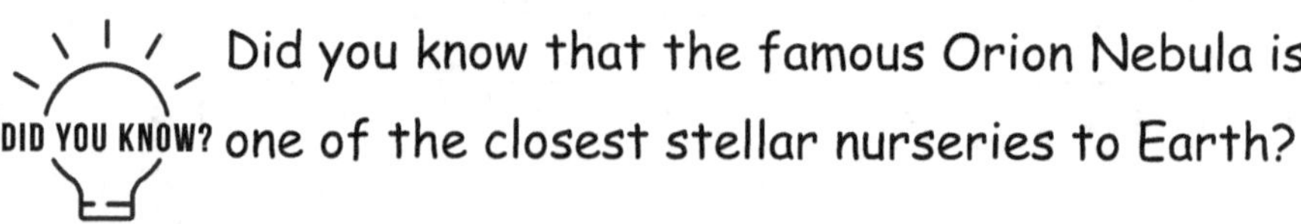

DID YOU KNOW? Did you know that the famous Orion Nebula is one of the closest stellar nurseries to Earth?

Quiz Question

2. What is the first stage of a star's life?

Options

A. White dwarf
B. Black hole
C. Supernova
D. Protostar

D. Protostar

The first stage of a star's life is the protostar phase. During this time, the gas and dust in a nebula collapse under gravity, increasing in temperature and pressure. Once nuclear fusion begins in the core, the protostar becomes a main-sequence star.

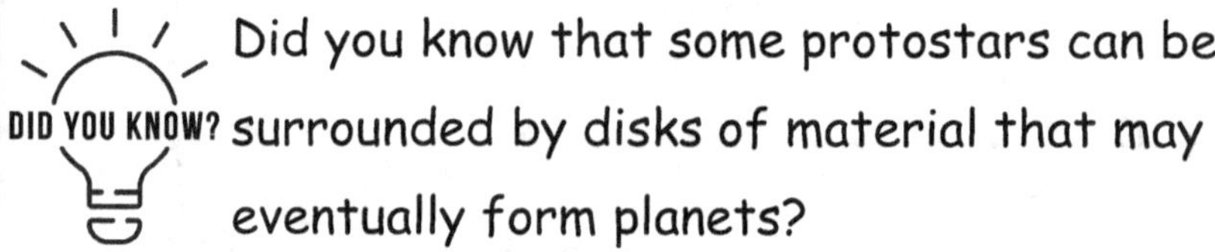

Did you know that some protostars can be surrounded by disks of material that may eventually form planets?

DID YOU KNOW?

Galactic Wonders: Birth of Stars

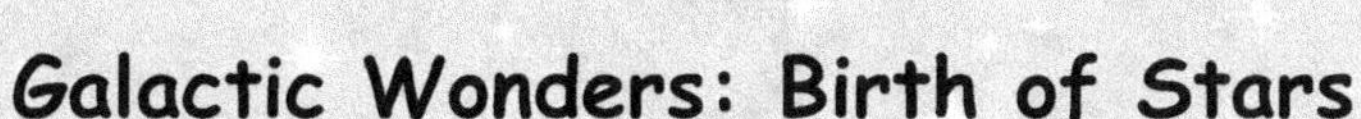

Quiz Question

3. What process powers a star?

Options

A. Chemical reactions
B. Nuclear fusion
C. Gravitational pull
D. Magnetic fields

B. Nuclear fusion

Stars are powered by nuclear fusion, a process in which hydrogen atoms combine to form helium, releasing a tremendous amount of energy. This energy radiates out, making the star shine brightly.

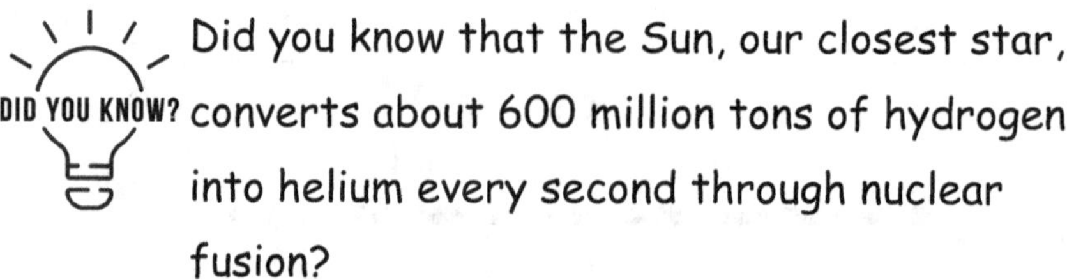

Did you know that the Sun, our closest star, converts about 600 million tons of hydrogen into helium every second through nuclear fusion?

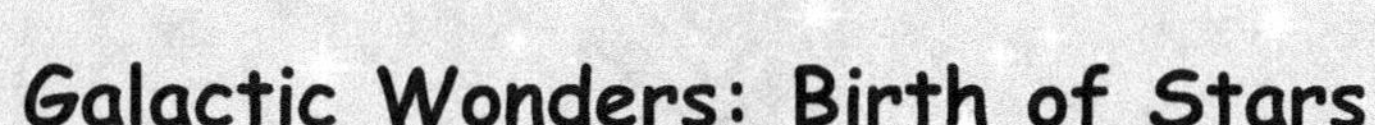

Quiz Question

4. What determines the color of a star?

Options

A. Distance from Earth

B. Age of the star

C. Temperature

D. Size

C. Temperature

The color of a star is determined by its temperature. Hotter stars appear blue or white, while cooler stars look red or orange. This difference in color is due to the varying wavelengths of light emitted by stars at different temperatures.

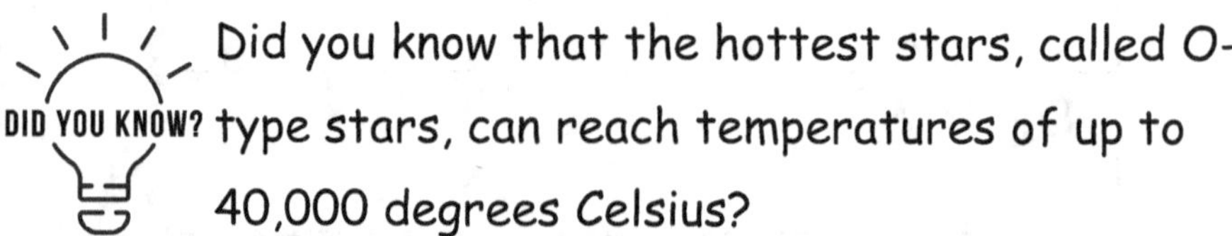

Did you know that the hottest stars, called O-type stars, can reach temperatures of up to 40,000 degrees Celsius?

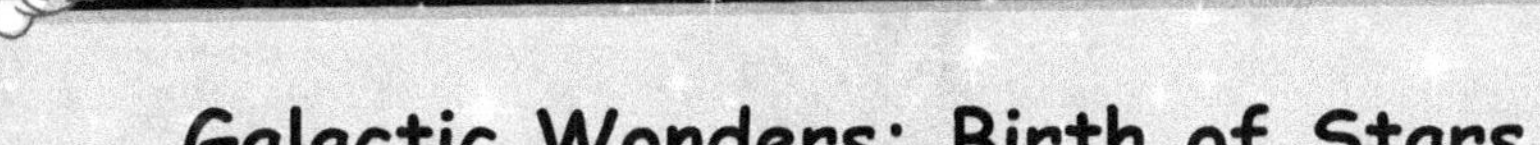

Quiz Question

5. What is the end stage of a massive star's life?

Options

A. Red giant

B. White dwarf

C. Neutron star or black hole

D. Protostar

C. Neutron star or black hole

The end stage of a massive star's life can result in either a neutron star or a black hole. When such a star exhausts its nuclear fuel, it undergoes a supernova explosion. The remaining core may collapse into a neutron star or, if massive enough, into a black hole.

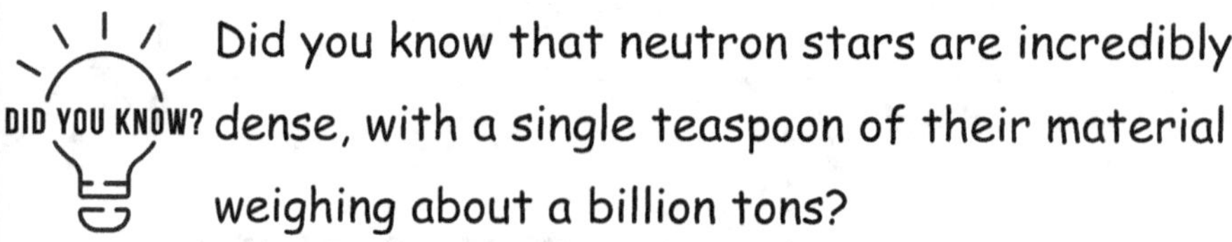

Did you know that neutron stars are incredibly dense, with a single teaspoon of their material weighing about a billion tons?

Quiz Question

1. What did ancient people often believe about the Milky Way?

Options

A. Ocean of stars
B. Pathway for spirits
C. Map of the world
D. Giant dragon

B. Pathway for spirits

Many ancient cultures believed that the Milky Way was a pathway for spirits. For example, the Greeks thought it was the road taken by the souls of the deceased to the afterlife. This mystical view linked the stars to the divine and the afterlife.

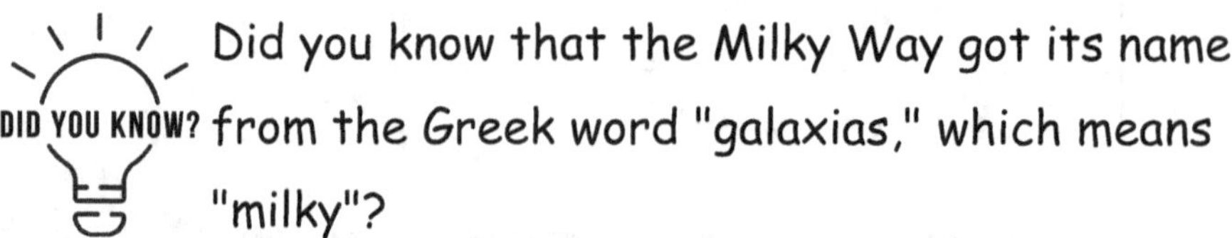

Did you know that the Milky Way got its name from the Greek word "galaxias," which means "milky"?

Quiz Question

2. How do constellations get their names?

Options

A. Random names

B. Astronomers' names

C. Mythological figures

D. Animal names

C. Mythological figures

Constellations are often named after mythological figures, animals, and objects. Ancient astronomers used these names to create stories and legends that explained the patterns they saw in the sky, making it easier to remember and navigate.

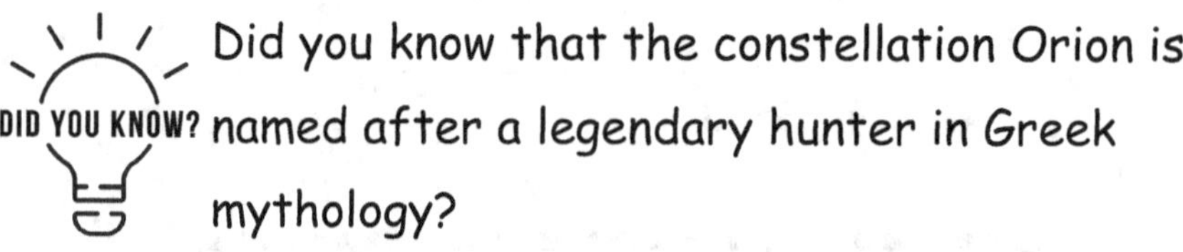

Did you know that the constellation Orion is named after a legendary hunter in Greek mythology?

Quiz Question

3. What is a supermoon?

Options

A.	Small moon
B.	Distant moon
C.	Closest full moon
D.	Moon eclipse

C. Closest full moon

A supermoon occurs when a full moon coincides with its closest approach to Earth in its orbit. This makes the moon appear larger and brighter than usual, creating a stunning sight in the night sky.

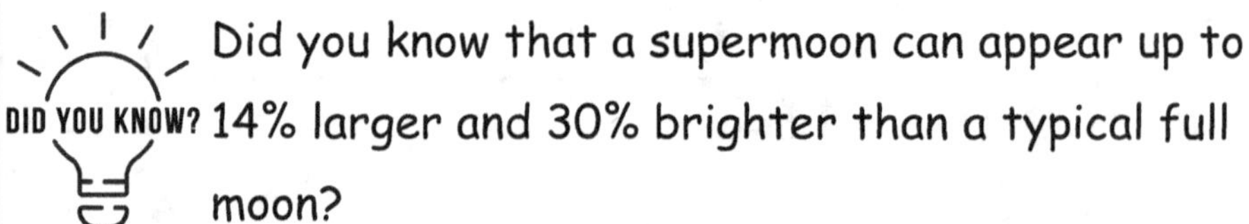

DID YOU KNOW? Did you know that a supermoon can appear up to 14% larger and 30% brighter than a typical full moon?

Space Stories: Magic and Mystery

Quiz Question

4. Why are black holes mysterious?

Options

A. Visible at night

B. Emit bright light

C. Impossible to see directly

D. Made of fire

C. Impossible to see directly

Black holes are mysterious because their immense gravity prevents anything, even light, from escaping. This makes them impossible to see directly with telescopes. Scientists study black holes by observing their effects on nearby matter and light.

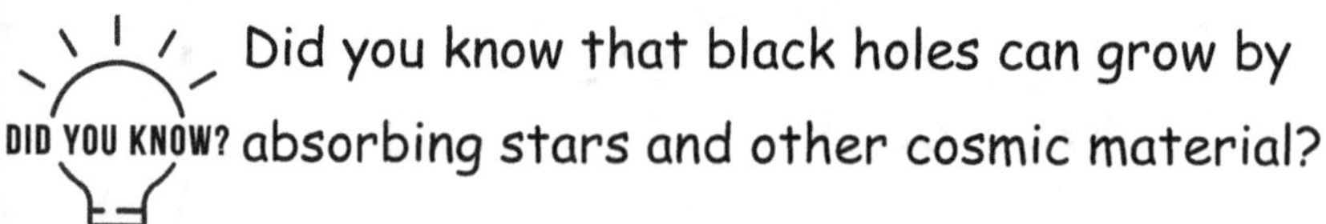

Did you know that black holes can grow by absorbing stars and other cosmic material?

Quiz Question

5. What is the oldest space object humans have observed?

Options

A. Moon

B. Earth

C. Sun

D. Universe's background radiation

D. Universe's background radiation

The oldest space object humans have observed is the cosmic microwave background radiation, which is the afterglow of the Big Bang. This radiation is over 13.8 billion years old and provides important clues about the early universe.

· · · · · · · · · · · · · · · · · · · ·

Did you know that studying the cosmic microwave background radiation has helped scientists understand the universe's age and composition?

1. What is the closest star system to our Solar System?

Options

| A. Alpha Centauri |
| B. Betelgeuse |
| C. Sirius |
| D. Proxima Centauri |

A. Alpha Centauri

The closest star system to our Solar System is Alpha Centauri, located about 4.37 light-years away. It consists of three stars: Alpha Centauri A, Alpha Centauri B, and Proxima Centauri, with Proxima Centauri being the closest to Earth. Understanding our closest cosmic neighbors helps scientists dream of interstellar travel and the possibility of visiting other star systems in the future.

• • • • • • • • • • • • • • • •

DID YOU KNOW? Fun Fact: Proxima Centauri, the nearest star to the Sun, has an exoplanet called Proxima b that may be in the habitable zone, where liquid water could exist!

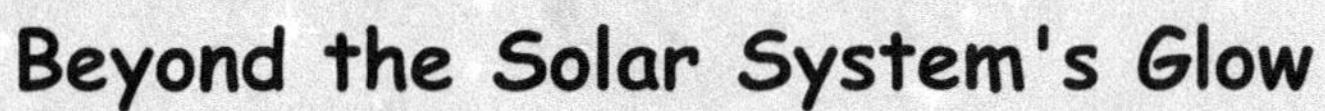

Quiz Question

2. What is the name of the boundary that marks the end of our Solar System?

Options

A. Kuiper Belt
B. Oort Cloud
C. Heliosphere
D. Asteroid Belt

C. Heliosphere

The Heliosphere is the bubble-like region of space dominated by the Sun's solar wind. It acts as a protective shield, marking the boundary where the solar wind's strength is no longer sufficient to push back against the interstellar medium. Beyond this boundary lies interstellar space, where the influence of our Sun diminishes.

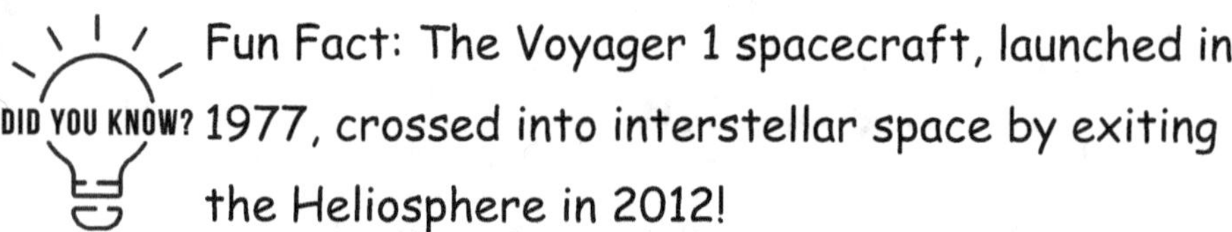

Fun Fact: The Voyager 1 spacecraft, launched in 1977, crossed into interstellar space by exiting the Heliosphere in 2012!

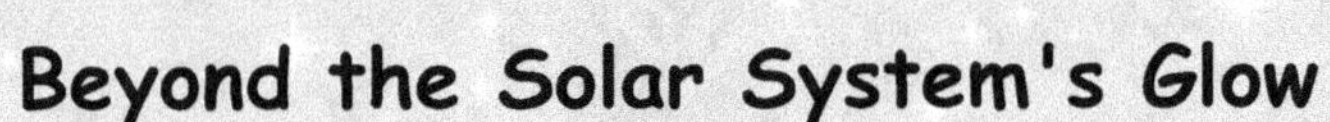

Quiz Question

3. Which spacecraft was the first to leave the Solar System?

Options

A. Pioneer 10

B. Voyager 1

C. New Horizons

D. Galileo

B. Voyager 1

Voyager 1, launched by NASA in 1977, became the first human-made object to leave the Solar System. It entered interstellar space in 2012, providing valuable data about the environment beyond the influence of our Sun. Even after decades, it continues to send information back to Earth, helping us explore the vastness beyond our Solar System.

· · · · · · · · · · · · · · · · · ·

DID YOU KNOW? Fun Fact: Voyager 1 carries a Golden Record with sounds and images from Earth, intended to communicate the story of our world to any potential extraterrestrial life!

Beyond the Solar System's Glow

Quiz Question

4. How far is the edge of the Solar System from the Sun?

Options

A. 93 million miles
B. 8 billion miles
C. 11 billion miles
D. 18 billion miles

D. 18 billion miles

The edge of the Solar System, specifically the outer boundary of the Heliosphere, is about 18 billion miles away from the Sun. This vast distance highlights the immense scale of our cosmic neighborhood. It takes spacecraft like Voyager 1 many years to travel such distances, showcasing the challenges and wonders of deep space exploration.

• • • • • • • • • • • • • • •

Fun Fact: It takes light from the Sun over 16 hours to reach the edge of the Solar System!

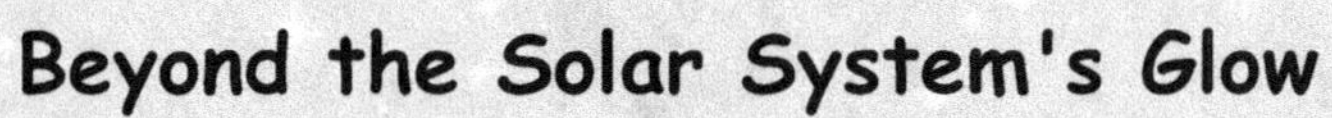

Beyond the Solar System's Glow

Quiz Question

5. What lies beyond the Solar System?

Options

A. The Milky Way
B. Asteroids
C. Comets
D. Pluto

A. The Milky Way

Beyond the Solar System lies the Milky Way galaxy, a vast collection of stars, planets, and cosmic phenomena. Our Solar System is just one of billions within this galaxy. Exploring beyond our Solar System gives us insights into the larger structure and mysteries of the universe, inspiring future generations to dream of distant worlds.

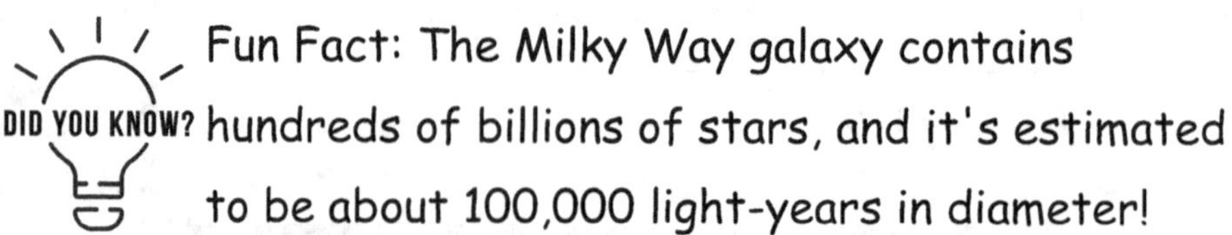

Fun Fact: The Milky Way galaxy contains hundreds of billions of stars, and it's estimated to be about 100,000 light-years in diameter!

Exploring Space, Where Dreams Flow

Quiz Question

1. What is the name of the first astronaut to walk on the Moon?

Options

A. Yuri Gagarin

B. Buzz Aldrin

C. Neil Armstrong

D. Michael Collins

C. Neil Armstrong

Neil Armstrong was the first astronaut to walk on the Moon during the Apollo 11 mission on July 20, 1969. His famous words, "That's one small step for man, one giant leap for mankind," marked a monumental moment in human history, showcasing our ability to explore beyond Earth and inspiring countless dreams of space travel.

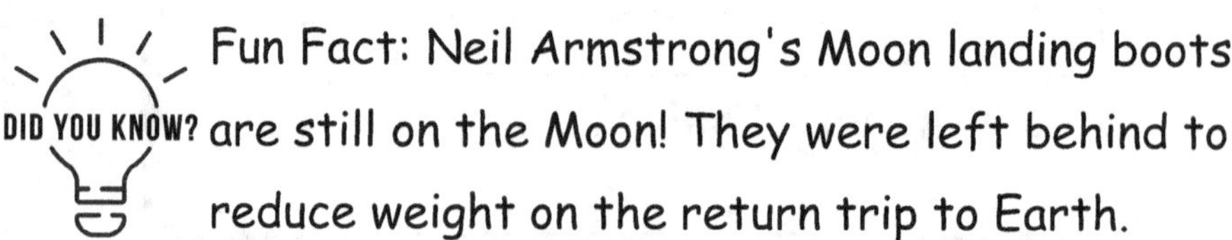

DID YOU KNOW? Fun Fact: Neil Armstrong's Moon landing boots are still on the Moon! They were left behind to reduce weight on the return trip to Earth.

Quiz Question

2. Which planet is known as the "Red Planet"?

Options

A. Venus
B. Earth
C. Mars
D. Jupiter

C. Mars

Mars is known as the "Red Planet" due to its reddish appearance, caused by iron oxide (rust) on its surface. Its unique color and proximity to Earth have made it a prime target for exploration, from robotic rovers to future human missions, igniting imagination and curiosity about potential life and human settlement on another planet.

• • • • • • • • • • • • • • • •

Fun Fact: Mars has the largest volcano in the Solar System, Olympus Mons, which is about 13.6 miles high—nearly three times the height of Mount Everest!

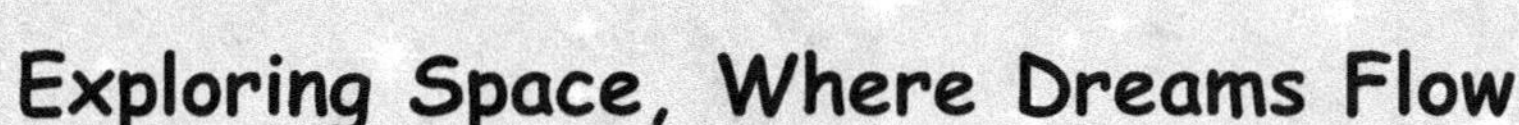

Quiz Question

3. What is the main goal of the International Space Station (ISS)?

Options

A. Military operations

B. Space tourism

C. Scientific research

D. Mining asteroids

C. Scientific research

The International Space Station (ISS) serves as a unique laboratory for scientific research in microgravity. Astronauts conduct experiments in various fields, including biology, physics, and astronomy, advancing our understanding of space and improving life on Earth. The ISS is a symbol of international cooperation, bringing together space agencies from around the world to work towards common scientific goals.

Fun Fact: The ISS travels around Earth at about 17,500 miles per hour, orbiting the planet approximately every 90 minutes!

Quiz Question

4. Which spacecraft was the first to land on Mars?

Options

A. Viking 1

B. Curiosity

C. Spirit

D. Opportunity

A. Viking 1

Viking 1, launched by NASA, was the first spacecraft to land successfully on Mars on July 20, 1976. It provided the first close-up images and scientific data from the Martian surface, paving the way for future missions and deepening our understanding of the Red Planet.

· · · · · · · · · · · · · · · · · · · ·

Fun Fact: The Viking missions helped confirm that Mars has soil chemistry that could support life, sparking ongoing debates and research about the possibility of life on Mars!

Quiz Question

5. What is the name of NASA's rover that landed on Mars in 2021?

Options

A. Spirit

B. Opportunity

C. Curiosity

D. Perseverance

D. Perseverance

NASA's Perseverance rover landed on Mars on February 18, 2021. Its mission includes searching for signs of past microbial life, collecting rock samples for future return to Earth, and testing new technology for future human exploration. Perseverance's advanced instruments and innovative technologies are paving the way for the next era of Mars exploration.

. . . .

Fun Fact: Perseverance carried a tiny helicopter named Ingenuity, which made the first powered flight on another planet!

The Edge of Universe, Secrets Bestow

Quiz Question

1. What is believed to be at the very edge of the universe?

Options

A. Stars
B. Black holes
C. Galaxies
D. Cosmic Microwave Background

D. Cosmic Microwave Background

The Cosmic Microwave Background (CMB) is the faint glow of radiation left over from the Big Bang, marking the edge of the observable universe. This ancient light provides a snapshot of the early universe, helping scientists understand its origins, structure, and evolution. The CMB's uniformity and minute fluctuations offer clues about the universe's composition and eventual fate.

• • • • • • • • • • • • • • • • • •

Fun Fact: The CMB is often referred to as the afterglow of the Big Bang, and it fills the universe almost uniformly with microwave radiation!

The Edge of Universe, Secrets Bestow

Quiz Question

2. What theory explains the origin of the universe?

Options

A. Steady State Theory

B. Big Bang Theory

C. String Theory

D. Quantum Theory

B. Big Bang Theory

The Big Bang Theory explains that the universe originated from an extremely hot and dense singularity approximately 13.8 billion years ago. This event caused the universe to expand and cool, eventually leading to the formation of galaxies, stars, and planets. The Big Bang Theory is supported by multiple lines of evidence, including the observation of the Cosmic Microwave Background.

• • • • • • • • • • • • • • • •

DID YOU KNOW? Fun Fact: The term "Big Bang" was actually coined as a derogatory term by British astronomer Fred Hoyle, who favored a different theory!

The Edge of Universe, Secrets Bestow

Quiz Question

3. How long does it take for light to travel from the edge of the observable universe to Earth?

Options

A. 1 million years

B. 13.8 million years

C. 4.3 billion years

D. 13.8 billion years

D. 13.8 billion years

Light from the edge of the observable universe takes about 13.8 billion years to reach Earth. This incredible distance means we are looking back in time when we observe distant celestial objects, seeing them as they were billions of years ago. Understanding these vast distances helps us comprehend the universe's immense scale and history.

Fun Fact: Because of the expanding universe, the actual distance to the edge of the observable universe is much larger than 13.8 billion light-years!

Quiz Question

4. What is a singularity in the context of black holes?

Options

A. A galaxy
B. A star
C. A point with infinite density
D. A planet

C. A point with infinite density

A singularity is a point within a black hole where gravitational forces compress matter to infinite density. It is where the known laws of physics break down. Studying singularities and black holes helps scientists explore extreme conditions and the fundamental nature of space, time, and gravity.

· · · · · · · · · · · · · · · ·

Fun Fact: The singularity at the center of a black hole is hidden by the event horizon, beyond which nothing, not even light, can escape!

5. What is dark energy believed to do to the universe?

Options

A. Slow it down

B. Stop it

C. Expand it

D. Shrink it

C. Expand it

Dark energy is a mysterious force that is believed to be driving the accelerated expansion of the universe. It makes up about 68% of the universe's total energy content. Understanding dark energy is one of the biggest challenges in cosmology, as it influences the universe's fate and helps explain why galaxies are moving away from each other at increasing speeds.

• • • • • • • • • • • • • • • • •

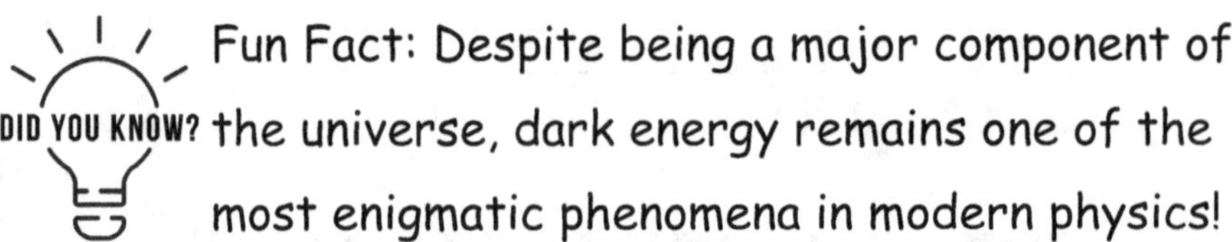

Fun Fact: Despite being a major component of the universe, dark energy remains one of the most enigmatic phenomena in modern physics!

Hubble's Wonders, Stars in a Row

1. What year was the Hubble Space Telescope launched?

Options

A. 1985

B. 1990

C. 1995

D. 2000

B. 1990

The Hubble Space Telescope was launched on April 24, 1990, aboard the Space Shuttle Discovery. It has since provided stunning images and valuable scientific data, revolutionizing our understanding of the universe. Hubble's observations have led to significant discoveries, including the accelerating expansion of the universe and the existence of exoplanets.

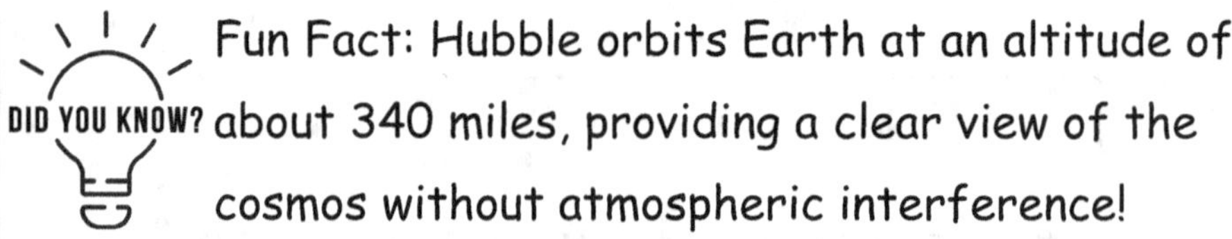

Fun Fact: Hubble orbits Earth at an altitude of about 340 miles, providing a clear view of the cosmos without atmospheric interference!

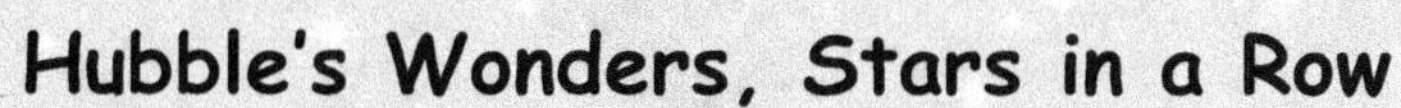

Hubble's Wonders, Stars in a Row

Quiz Question

2. What is one of the most famous images captured by Hubble?

Options

A. Pillars of Creation

B. Martian Surface

C. Moon Landing

D. Earth's core

A. Pillars of Creation

The "Pillars of Creation" is one of Hubble's most iconic images, showcasing towering columns of gas and dust in the Eagle Nebula, where new stars are being born. This image highlights the beauty and complexity of stellar nurseries, inspiring awe and wonder about the processes that create stars and planetary systems.

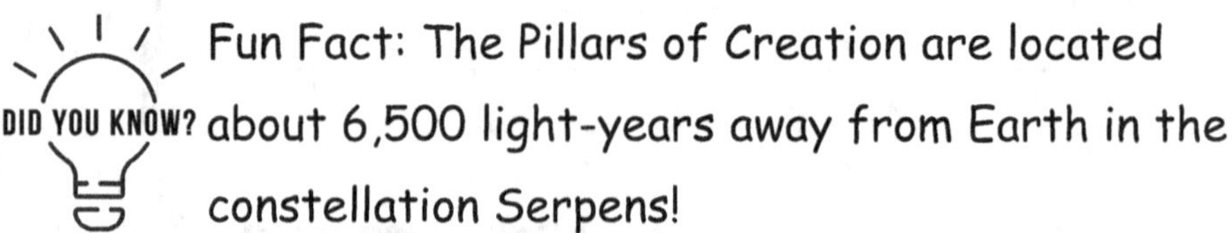

Fun Fact: The Pillars of Creation are located about 6,500 light-years away from Earth in the constellation Serpens!

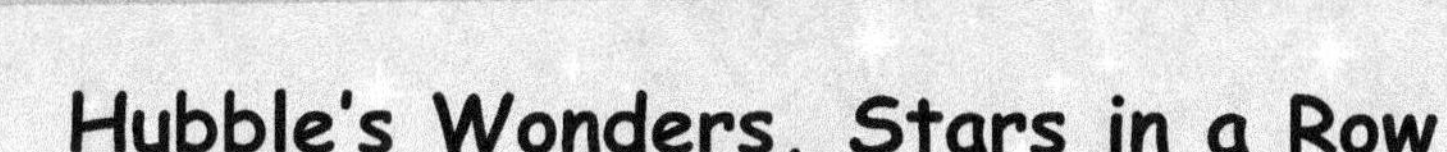

Quiz Question

3. Which planet's moons did Hubble help discover?

Options

A. Mars

B. Jupiter

C. Saturn

D. Neptune

D. Neptune

Hubble helped discover new moons around Neptune, including one named Hippocamp. These discoveries enhance our understanding of the outer planets and their diverse satellite systems. Hubble's ability to observe distant objects with incredible detail has made it an invaluable tool for planetary science.

• • • • • • • • • • • • • • • •

DID YOU KNOW? Fun Fact: Neptune's moon Hippocamp is named after a mythological sea creature, fitting for a moon orbiting a planet named after the Roman god of the sea!

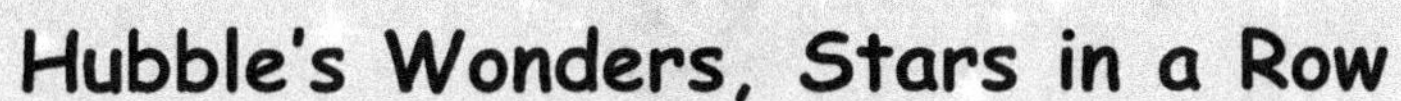

4. How many galaxies are estimated to be in the observable universe, based on Hubble's observations?

Options

A. 100 million
B. 1 billion
C. 100 billion
D. 1 trillion

C. 100 billion

Based on Hubble's observations, scientists estimate that there are about 100 billion galaxies in the observable universe. Each galaxy contains millions or even billions of stars, highlighting the vastness and richness of the cosmos. This mind-boggling number encourages curiosity and exploration, as we strive to understand our place in the universe.

Fun Fact: The Hubble Deep Field images, taken in the mid-1990s, revealed thousands of galaxies in a tiny patch of sky, transforming our understanding of the universe's scale!

Quiz Question

1. What is the primary mission of the James Webb Space Telescope (JWST)?

Options

A. Study Earth's core
B. Explore the Sun
C. Observe the early universe
D. Track asteroids

C. Observe the early universe

The primary mission of the James Webb Space Telescope (JWST) is to observe the early universe, focusing on the formation of stars and galaxies shortly after the Big Bang. With its advanced infrared capabilities, JWST will peer deeper into space and time than ever before, providing unprecedented insights into the cosmos' origins and evolution.

• • • • • • • • • • • • • • • • • •

Fun Fact: JWST is equipped with a massive sunshield the size of a tennis court to protect its instruments from the Sun's heat, ensuring optimal performance!

Quiz Question

2. How does JWST compare to the Hubble Space Telescope?

Options

A. Smaller mirror

B. Lower resolution

C. Infrared capabilities

D. No difference

C. Infrared capabilities

Unlike Hubble, which primarily observes in visible and ultraviolet light, JWST is designed to observe in the infrared spectrum. This allows it to see through cosmic dust clouds and detect faint objects, such as distant galaxies and exoplanets, providing a clearer view of the universe's early stages and detailed studies of planetary atmospheres.

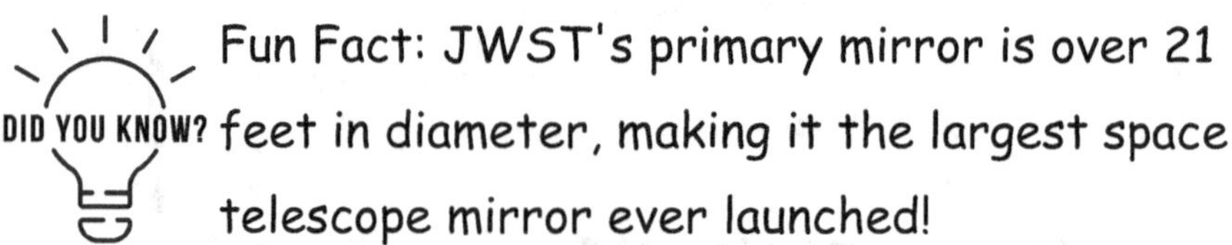

Fun Fact: JWST's primary mirror is over 21 feet in diameter, making it the largest space telescope mirror ever launched!

Quiz Question

1. Who was the first human to journey into outer space?

Options

A. John Glenn
B. Neil Armstrong
C. Yuri Gagarin
D. Buzz Aldrin

C. Yuri Gagarin

Yuri Gagarin made history on April 12, 1961, by becoming the first human to travel into space. His spacecraft, Vostok 1, completed an orbit of Earth in 108 minutes, a monumental achievement during the Space Race. This voyage demonstrated that humans could survive and work in space, paving the way for future exploration. Yuri's bravery and the mission's success ignited imaginations worldwide.

• • • • • • • • • • • • • • • •

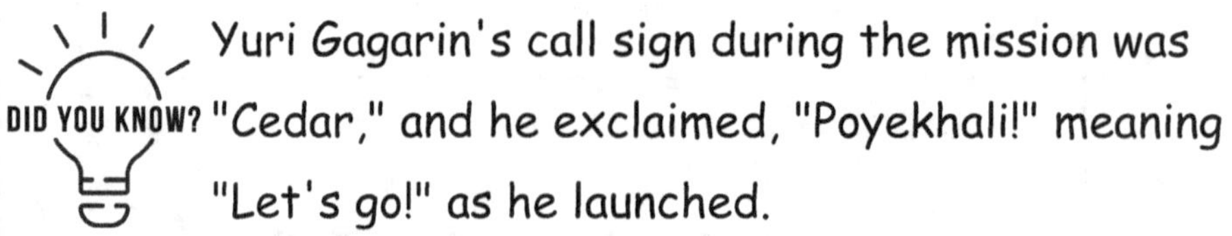

DID YOU KNOW? Yuri Gagarin's call sign during the mission was "Cedar," and he exclaimed, "Poyekhali!" meaning "Let's go!" as he launched.

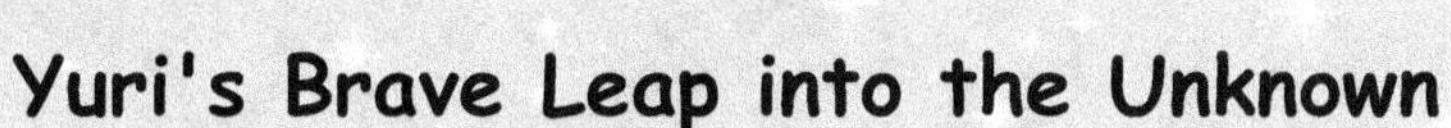

Quiz Question

2. What was the name of Yuri Gagarin's spacecraft?

Options

A. Apollo 11
B. Vostok 1
C. Soyuz 1
D. Sputnik 1

B. Vostok 1

Vostok 1 was the spacecraft that carried Yuri Gagarin into orbit. It was part of the Soviet Vostok program, designed to determine if humans could endure spaceflight. Vostok 1 was a spherical capsule, which provided a safe environment for Gagarin to experience the rigors of space. This mission was a significant milestone in human space exploration.

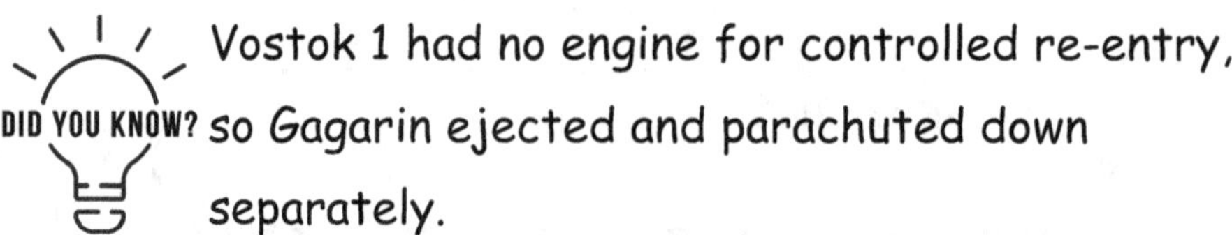

DID YOU KNOW? Vostok 1 had no engine for controlled re-entry, so Gagarin ejected and parachuted down separately.

Neil's Footsteps on the Moon's Dusty Throne

Quiz Question

1. Who was the first human to walk on the moon?

Options

A. Yuri Gagarin

B. Buzz Aldrin

C. John Glenn

D. Neil Armstrong

D. Neil Armstrong

Neil Armstrong became the first human to walk on the moon on July 20, 1969, during NASA's Apollo 11 mission. His famous words, "That's one small step for man, one giant leap for mankind," marked this incredible achievement. Armstrong's moonwalk symbolized humanity's ability to overcome challenges and reach for the stars.

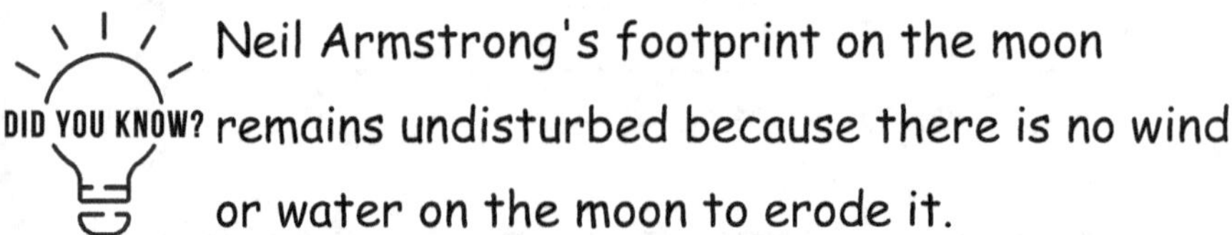

Neil Armstrong's footprint on the moon remains undisturbed because there is no wind or water on the moon to erode it.

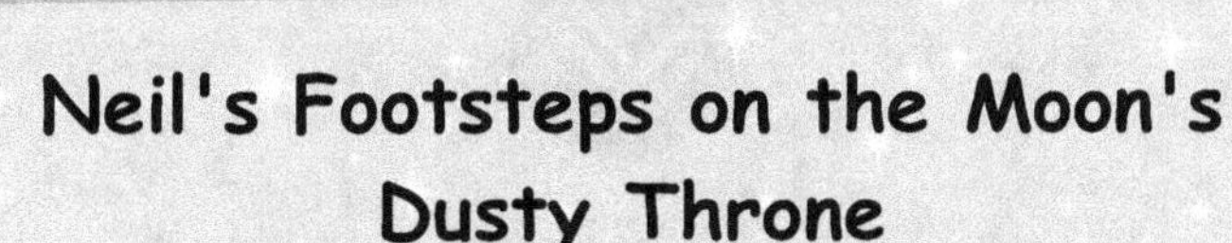

Quiz Question

2. What was the name of the lunar module that carried Neil Armstrong and Buzz Aldrin to the moon's surface?

Options

A. Eagle
B. Falcon
C. Hawk
D. Phoenix

A. Eagle

The lunar module for Apollo 11 was named "Eagle."
Armstrong and Aldrin used Eagle to descend from the
command module and land on the moon's surface in the
Sea of Tranquility. The name echoed the mission's
spirit of exploration and American pride, as the bald
eagle is the national bird of the United States.

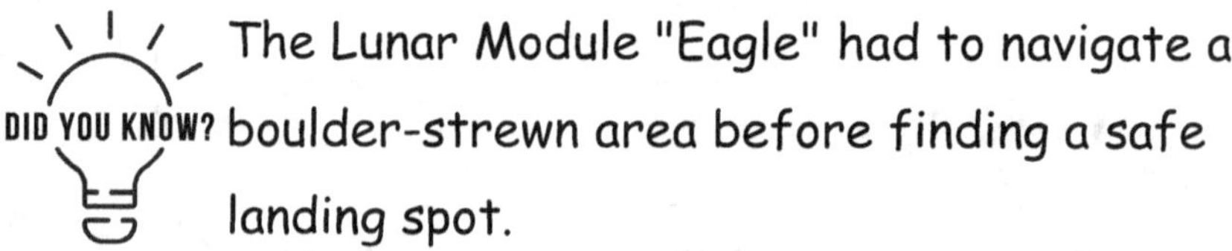

DID YOU KNOW? The Lunar Module "Eagle" had to navigate a
boulder-strewn area before finding a safe
landing spot.

Quiz Question

3. How long did Neil Armstrong and Buzz Aldrin spend walking on the moon?

Options

A. 1 hour
B. 2 hours
C. 3 hours
D. 2.5 hours

D. 2.5 hours

Armstrong and Aldrin spent approximately 2.5 hours walking on the moon, conducting experiments, collecting samples, and exploring the lunar terrain. Their activities provided invaluable data and insights into the moon's composition and environment. This historic moonwalk was a testament to human ingenuity and determination.

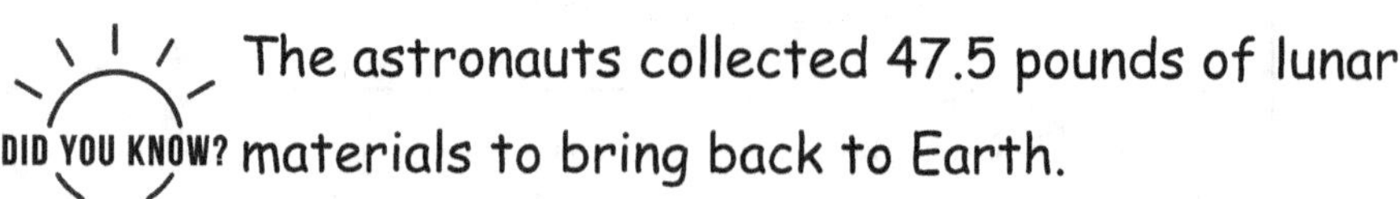

The astronauts collected 47.5 pounds of lunar materials to bring back to Earth.

Quiz Question

1. Who was the first American woman to travel to space?

Options

A. Mae Jemison
B. Sally Ride
C. Valentina Tereshkova
D. Peggy Whitson

B. Sally Ride

Sally Ride became the first American woman to travel to space on June 18, 1983, aboard the Space Shuttle Challenger. As a mission specialist on STS-7, Ride's work included deploying satellites and conducting scientific experiments. Her journey inspired countless young girls to pursue careers in science and space exploration.

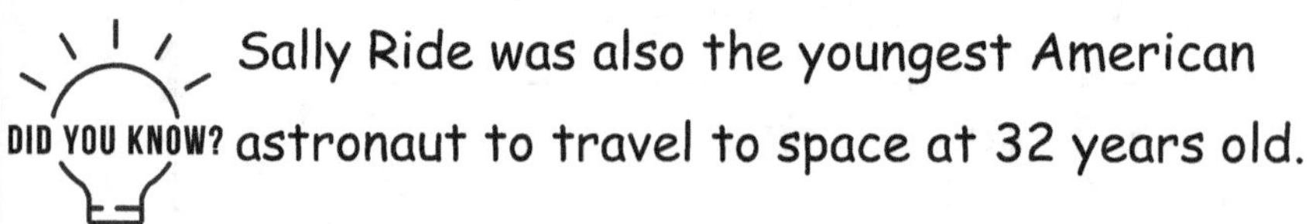

DID YOU KNOW? Sally Ride was also the youngest American astronaut to travel to space at 32 years old.

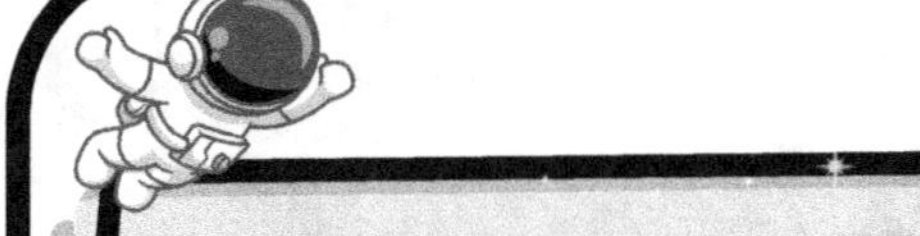

Quiz Question

2. Which space shuttle did Sally Ride fly on for her historic mission?

Options

| A. Atlantis |
| B. Endeavour |
| C. Discovery |
| D. Challenger |

D. Challenger

Sally Ride flew aboard the Space Shuttle Challenger for her historic mission, STS-7. Challenger played a crucial role in the Space Shuttle program, and Ride's participation marked a significant milestone in gender equality and opportunities for women in space.

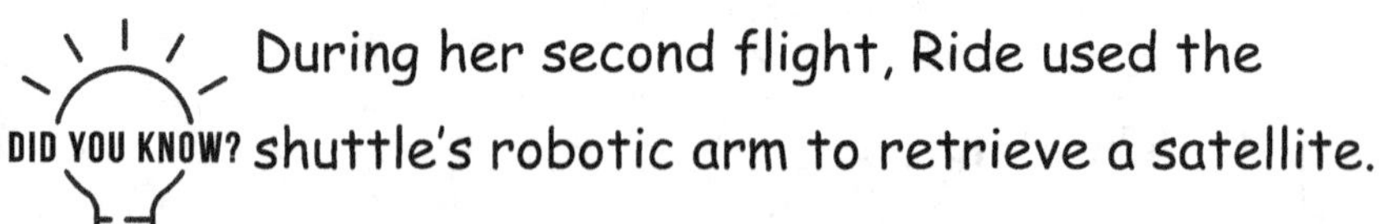

During her second flight, Ride used the shuttle's robotic arm to retrieve a satellite.

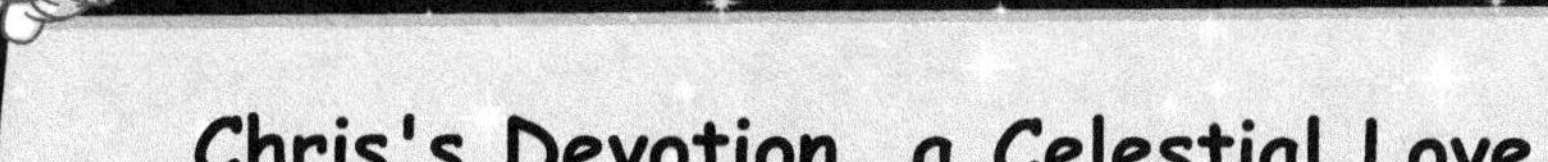

Chris's Devotion, a Celestial Love

Quiz Question

1. What nationality is astronaut Chris Hadfield?

Options

A. American
B. British
C. Canadian
D. Australian

C. Canadian

Chris Hadfield is a Canadian astronaut known for his charismatic personality and contributions to space exploration. He became the first Canadian to command the International Space Station (ISS). His engaging presence on social media and educational outreach have made him a beloved figure in space science.

· · · · · · · · · · · · · · · · · · ·

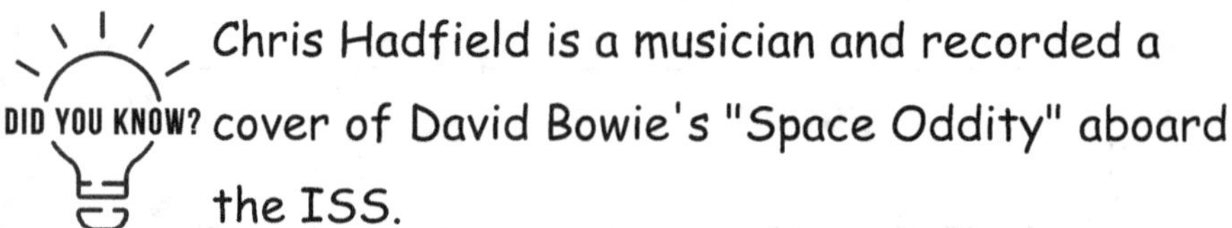

DID YOU KNOW? Chris Hadfield is a musician and recorded a cover of David Bowie's "Space Oddity" aboard the ISS.

Quiz Question

2. How many spacewalks has Chris Hadfield performed?

Options

A. 1

B. 2

C. 3

D. 4

C. 3

Chris Hadfield has conducted three spacewalks during his missions. These extravehicular activities (EVAs) involved performing maintenance and upgrades on the ISS, showcasing his technical skills and dedication to advancing human space exploration. His spacewalks contributed to the ongoing functionality and success of the ISS.

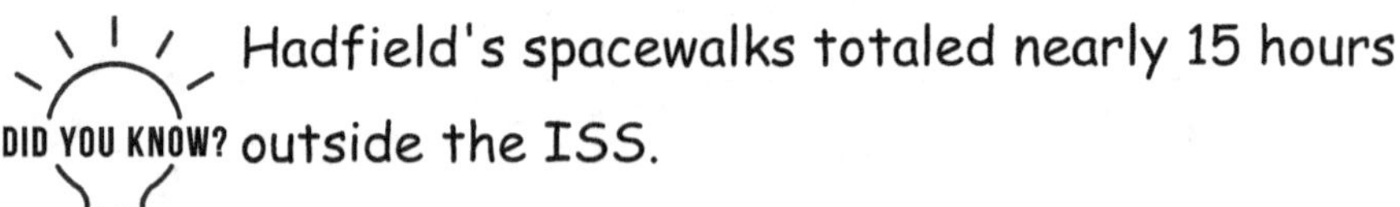

DID YOU KNOW? Hadfield's spacewalks totaled nearly 15 hours outside the ISS.

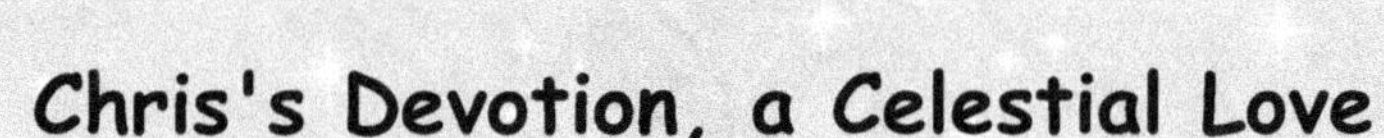

Quiz Question

3. What was Chris Hadfield's role on his last space mission?

Options

A. Pilot

B. Scientist

C. Commander

D. Engineer

C. Commander

On his last space mission, Chris Hadfield served as the commander of the ISS. As commander, he led the crew in conducting scientific research, maintaining the station, and engaging with the public through social media and educational outreach. His leadership and dedication were instrumental in the mission's success.

• • • • • • • • • • • • • • • •

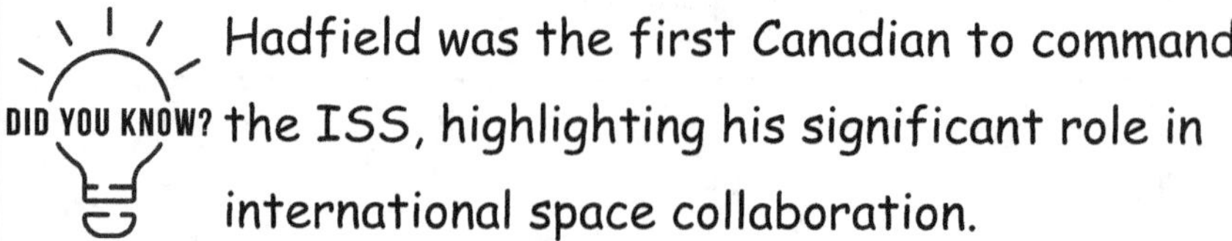

Hadfield was the first Canadian to command the ISS, highlighting his significant role in international space collaboration.

Pioneers Together, Reaching New Heights

Quiz Question

1. What is one common goal of space missions conducted by different countries?

Options

A. Collecting alien specimens

B. Dominating space

C. Advancing scientific knowledge

D. Finding new planets to live on

C. Advancing scientific knowledge

A common goal of space missions is to advance scientific knowledge. Whether it's studying the effects of microgravity, exploring other planets, or developing new technologies, space missions contribute to understanding our universe and improving life on Earth.

• • • • • • • • • • • • • • • • • • •

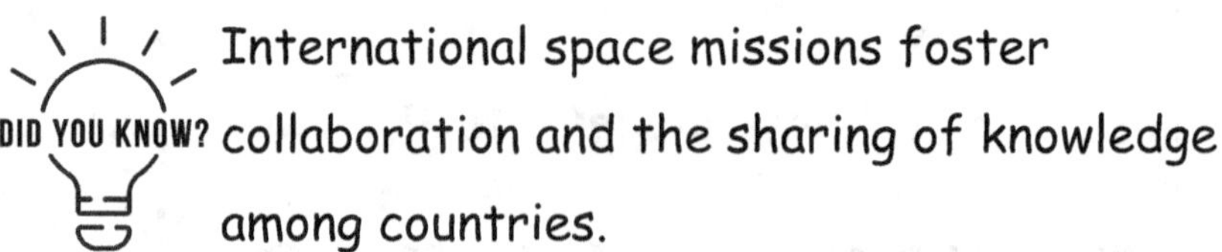

International space missions foster collaboration and the sharing of knowledge among countries.

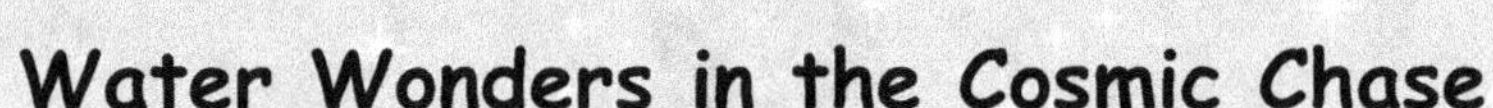

Water Wonders in the Cosmic Chase

Quiz Question

1. What is the most common form that water takes in outer space?

Options

A. Liquid

B. Gas

C. Ice

D. Plasma

C. Ice

In outer space, the most common form of water is ice. Due to the extremely low temperatures, water freezes instantly and can be found as ice on celestial bodies like moons and asteroids. The vacuum of space and lack of atmosphere prevent water from existing in liquid form, making ice the prevalent state we discover.

• • • • • • • • • • • • • • • • •

DID YOU KNOW? Fun Fact: Did you know that scientists believe some asteroids are made up of nearly 50% water ice?

Water Wonders in the Cosmic Chase

Quiz Question

2. How do astronomers identify water on distant planets?

Options

A. Microscopes
B. Telescopes
C. Space probes
D. Radio waves

B. Telescopes

Astronomers use telescopes equipped with special instruments to identify water on distant planets. By analyzing the light spectra emitted or absorbed by a planet, they can detect the presence of water vapor, ice, or liquid water. These spectral "fingerprints" help scientists understand a planet's composition and potential for life.

Fun Fact: The Hubble Space Telescope has been instrumental in discovering water vapor in the atmospheres of exoplanets!

Quiz Question

3. What role does water play in the search for extraterrestrial life?

Options

A. Aesthetic Value

B. Essential for Technology

C. Potential Habitat

D. Energy Source

C. Potential Habitat

Water is crucial in the search for extraterrestrial life because it is a fundamental ingredient for life as we know it. Scientists believe that wherever there is water, there might also be life. This drives missions to places like Mars and Europa, where water exists or once existed, to search for signs of life.

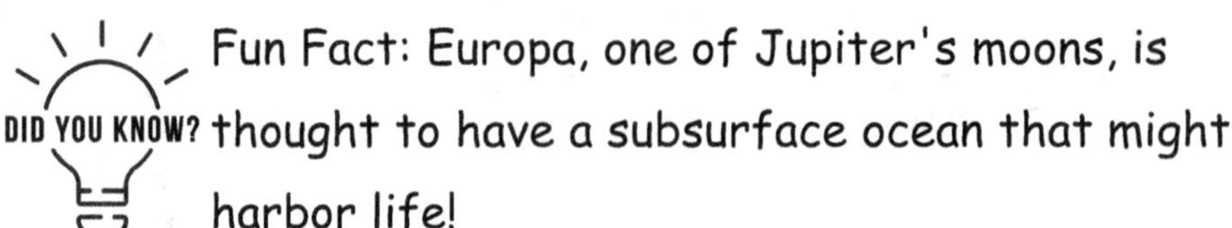

Fun Fact: Europa, one of Jupiter's moons, is thought to have a subsurface ocean that might harbor life!

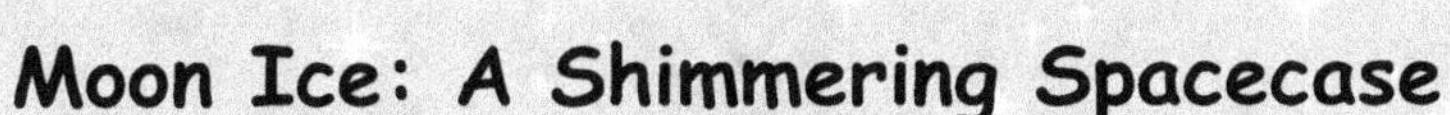

Moon Ice: A Shimmering Spacecase

1. Where on the Moon has water ice been found?

Options

A. In craters at the poles
B. On the highlands
C. In the maria
D. On the surface everywhere

A. In craters at the poles

Water ice has been found in the permanently shadowed craters at the Moon's poles. These craters never receive sunlight, allowing the ice to remain frozen. This discovery is significant as it highlights the possibility of using lunar water ice for future space missions and even human settlements on the Moon.

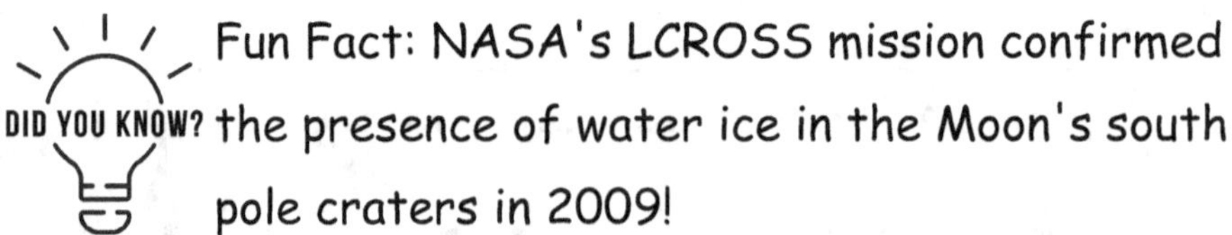

Fun Fact: NASA's LCROSS mission confirmed the presence of water ice in the Moon's south pole craters in 2009!

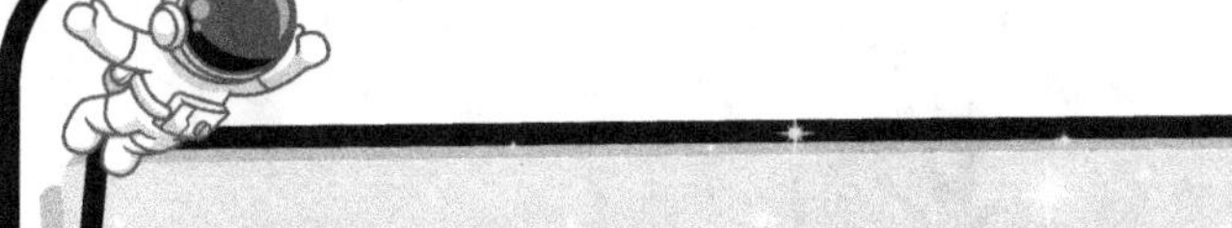

Quiz Question

2. How do scientists believe water arrived on the Moon?

Options

A. From lunar volcanoes
B. From solar wind
C. From comets and asteroids
D. From Earth's oceans

C. From comets and asteroids

Scientists think that water on the Moon was delivered by comets and asteroids that collided with its surface. These celestial bodies contained ice, which got deposited in the cold, shadowed regions. Over billions of years, this water remained frozen in the Moon's craters.

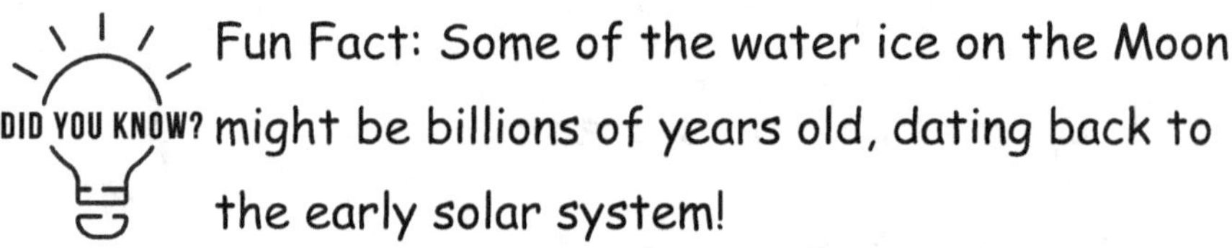

Fun Fact: Some of the water ice on the Moon might be billions of years old, dating back to the early solar system!

Moon Ice: A Shimmering Spacecase

Quiz Question

3. What potential uses does lunar ice have for future astronauts?

Options

A. Making jewelry

B. Fuel production

C. Entertainment

D. Art projects

B. Fuel production

Lunar ice can be split into hydrogen and oxygen to produce rocket fuel and also provide drinking water and breathable oxygen for astronauts. This makes it a vital resource for sustaining human presence and facilitating deep space exploration.

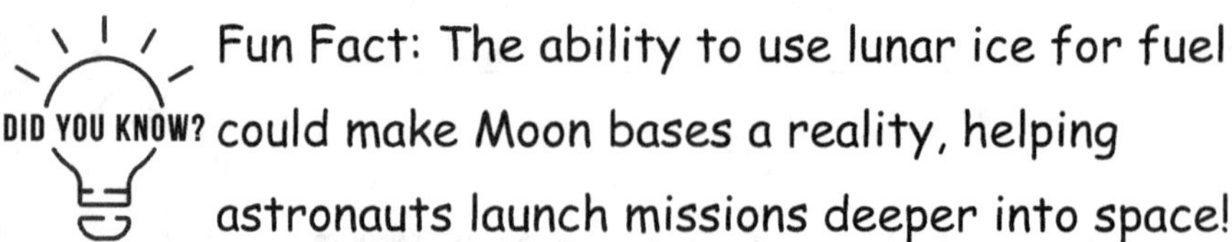

Fun Fact: The ability to use lunar ice for fuel could make Moon bases a reality, helping astronauts launch missions deeper into space!

Quiz Question

4. What is a major challenge in extracting ice from the Moon?

Options

A. Lack of technology

B. High temperatures

C. Low gravity

D. Extreme cold and darkness

D. Extreme cold and darkness

One of the major challenges in extracting ice from the Moon is dealing with the extreme cold and darkness in the permanently shadowed craters where the ice is located. These areas can be incredibly cold, making it difficult to design equipment that can operate effectively.

· · · · · · · · · · · · · · · · · ·

DID YOU KNOW? Fun Fact: Temperatures in the Moon's shadowed craters can drop to -250 degrees Fahrenheit, making them some of the coldest places in the solar system!

Moon Ice: A Shimmering Spacecase

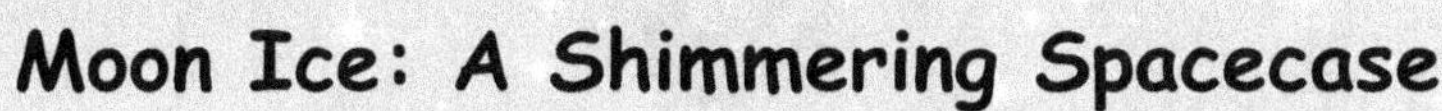

Quiz Question

5. Why is the discovery of water ice on the Moon considered a game-changer for space exploration?

Options

A. It proves aliens exist
B. It makes the Moon more colorful
C. It supports sustainable exploration
D. It generates income

C. It supports sustainable exploration

The discovery of water ice on the Moon is a game-changer because it provides a sustainable resource for long-term space exploration. Water can support life, generate fuel, and help establish lunar bases, making it a cornerstone for future missions beyond Earth.

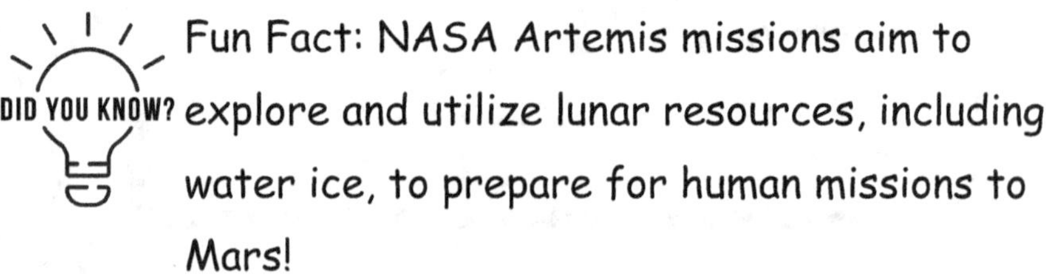

Fun Fact: NASA Artemis missions aim to explore and utilize lunar resources, including water ice, to prepare for human missions to Mars!

Quiz Question

1. Where is most of the water on Mars found?

Options

A. In the atmosphere

B. On the surface

C. In polar ice caps

D. In underground lakes

C. In polar ice caps

Most of the known water on Mars is found in its polar ice caps, which are made of water ice and dry ice (frozen carbon dioxide). These ice caps shrink and grow with the Martian seasons, revealing the dynamic nature of Mars's climate.

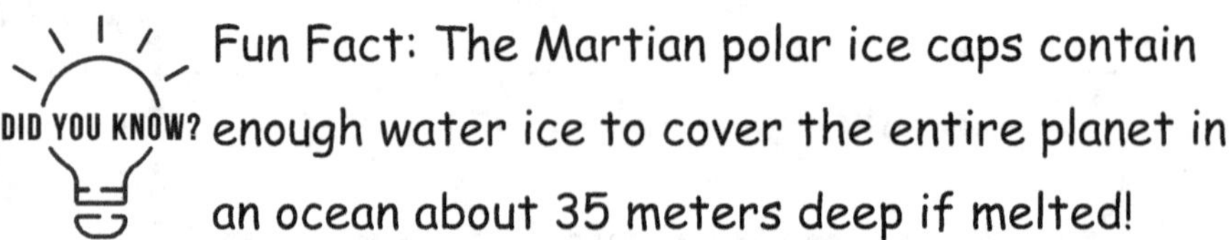

Fun Fact: The Martian polar ice caps contain enough water ice to cover the entire planet in an ocean about 35 meters deep if melted!

Mars's Frosty Hidden Place

Quiz Question

2. What is a significant indicator of liquid water on Mars?

Options

A. Dust storms

B. Seasonal dark streaks

C. Red soil

D. High mountains

B. Seasonal dark streaks

Seasonal dark streaks, known as recurring slope lineae (RSL), are considered a significant indicator of liquid water on Mars. These streaks appear during warmer seasons and fade away when it's colder, suggesting that they might be formed by salty liquid water flows.

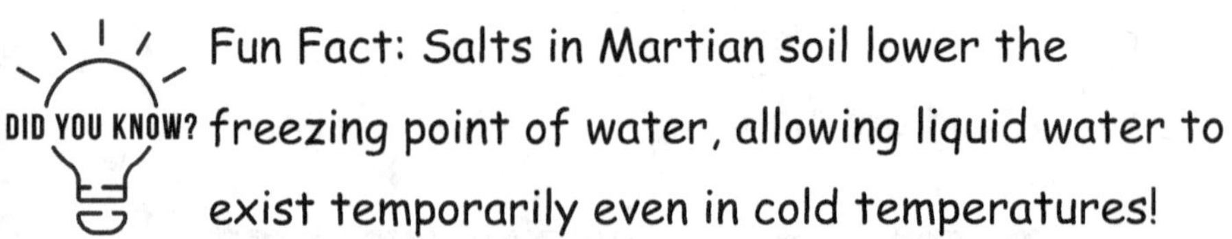

Fun Fact: Salts in Martian soil lower the freezing point of water, allowing liquid water to exist temporarily even in cold temperatures!

DID YOU KNOW?

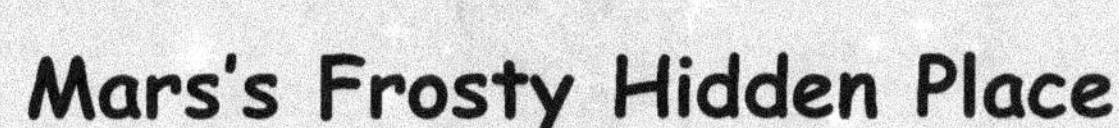

Quiz Question

3. How is water thought to have disappeared from Mars's surface?

Options

A. Absorbed by rocks

B. Evaporated into space

C. Turned into crystals

D. Consumed by Martians

B. Evaporated into space

Water on Mars is believed to have evaporated into space due to the planet's thin atmosphere. Over millions of years, solar winds stripped away the atmosphere, causing water to escape into space and leaving the planet dry and barren.

• • • • • • • • • • • • • • • • • •

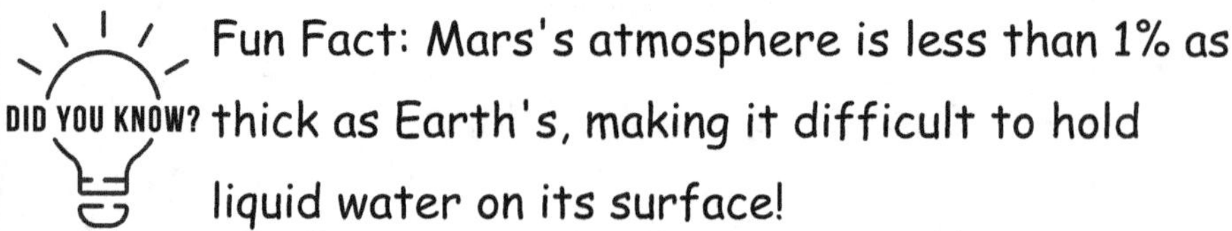

Fun Fact: Mars's atmosphere is less than 1% as thick as Earth's, making it difficult to hold liquid water on its surface!

Mars's Frosty Hidden Place

Quiz Question

4. What recent discovery hints at underground water on Mars?

Options

A. Lava flows
B. Underground lake beneath the south pole
C. Sand dunes
D. Martian canals

B. Underground lake beneath the south pole

Radar data from Mars Express suggested the existence of an underground lake beneath the south pole of Mars. This discovery hints at the possibility of liquid water existing below the surface, potentially creating a habitable environment for microbial life.

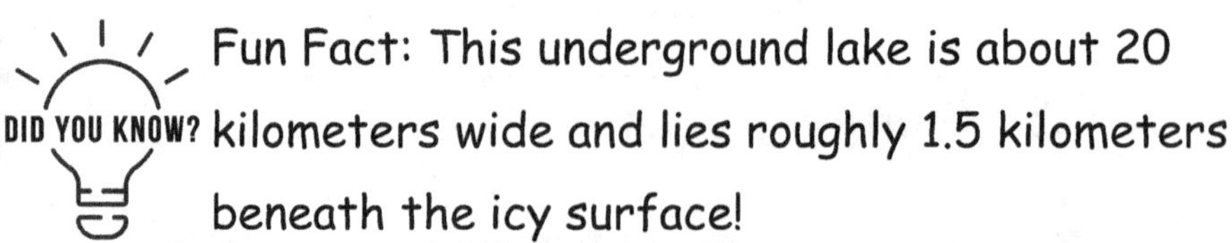

Fun Fact: This underground lake is about 20 kilometers wide and lies roughly 1.5 kilometers beneath the icy surface!

Mars's Frosty Hidden Place

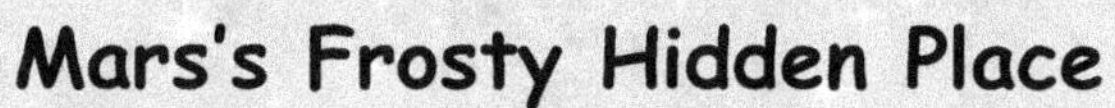

Quiz Question

5. Why is water important for future human missions to Mars?

Options

A. For cooling equipment

B. For aesthetic beauty

C. For drinking and fuel

D. For painting landscapes

C. For drinking and fuel

Water is critical for future human missions to Mars because it can provide drinking water, support agriculture, and be split into hydrogen and oxygen for fuel. Access to water would make long-term human presence on Mars feasible and sustainable.

• • • • • • • • • • • • • • • • • •

DID YOU KNOW? Fun Fact: Future missions may use technology to extract water from the Martian soil, which contains small amounts of water per cubic meter!

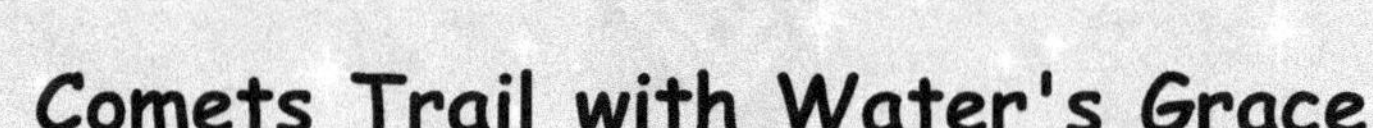

Comets Trail with Water's Grace

Quiz Question

1. What are comets primarily made of?

Options

A. Rock and dust
B. Metal and gas
C. Ice and dust
D. Fire and magma

C. Ice and dust

Comets are primarily made of ice, dust, and rocky material. These "dirty snowballs" travel through space and develop glowing comas and tails when they get close to the Sun. The heat causes the ice to vaporize, creating a spectacular display.

• • • • • • • • • • • • • • • •

DID YOU KNOW? Fun Fact: The nucleus of a comet, its solid core, can be as small as a few hundred meters or as large as tens of kilometers in diameter!

Comets Trail with Water's Grace

Quiz Question

2. What happens to a comet as it approaches the Sun?

Options

A. It freezes solid

B. It breaks apart

C. It forms a glowing coma and tail

D. It becomes invisible

C. It forms a glowing coma and tail

As a comet approaches the Sun, the heat causes its ice to vaporize and release gas and dust. This forms a glowing coma around the nucleus and a tail that always points away from the Sun due to the solar wind.

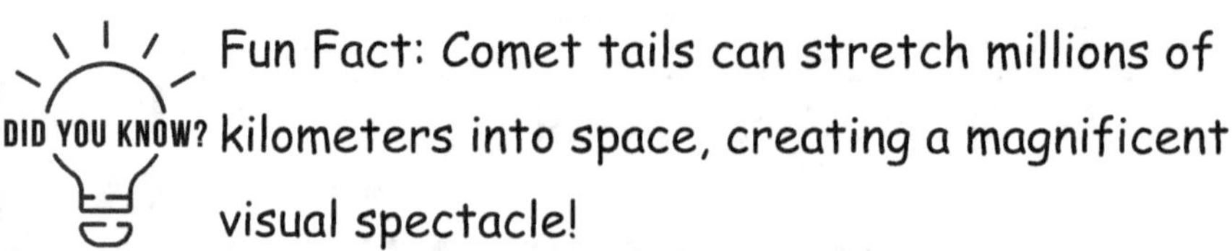

Fun Fact: Comet tails can stretch millions of kilometers into space, creating a magnificent visual spectacle!

Comets Trail with Water's Grace

Quiz Question

3. What is the significance of water in comets?

Options

A. It makes them colorful

B. It's a potential source of water for planets

C. It makes them fly faster

D. It makes them spherical

B. It's a potential source of water for planets

The ice in comets is significant because it is a potential source of water for planets. Some scientists believe that comets may have delivered water to Earth in its early history, contributing to the formation of our oceans.

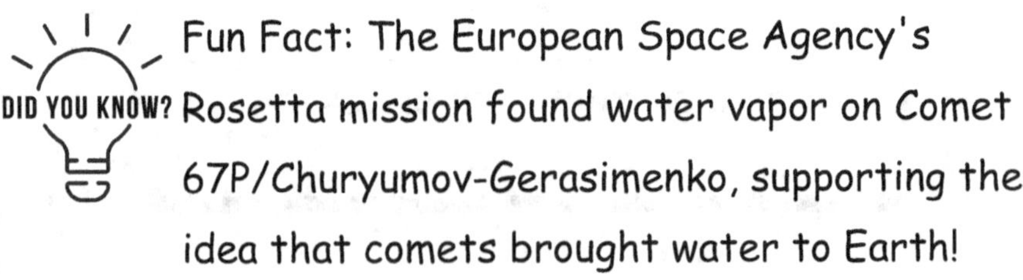

· · · · · · · · · · · · · · · ·

Fun Fact: The European Space Agency's Rosetta mission found water vapor on Comet 67P/Churyumov-Gerasimenko, supporting the idea that comets brought water to Earth!

Quiz Question

4. How do scientists study comets?

Options

A. By looking at them through telescopes
B. By landing spacecraft on them
C. By sending probes to fly by them
D. All of the above

D. All of the above

Scientists study comets by using telescopes to observe them, sending probes to fly by them, and even landing spacecraft on their surface. These methods help us understand the composition, structure, and behavior of comets.

• • • • • • • • • • • • • • •

Fun Fact: The first successful landing on a comet was achieved by the Rosetta mission's Philae lander in 2014!

Comets Trail with Water's Grace

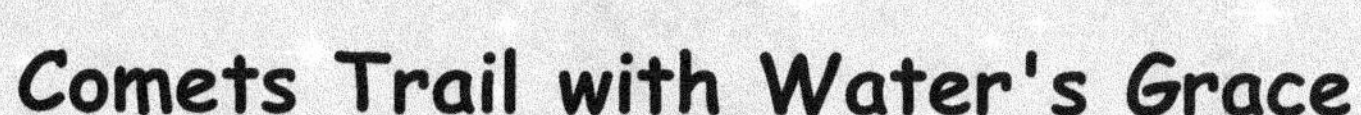

Quiz Question

5. What famous comet can be seen from Earth approximately every 76 years?

Options

A. Halley's Comet

B. Comet Hale-Bopp

C. Comet Encke

D. Comet Tempel-Tuttle

A. Halley's Comet

Halley's Comet is the most famous comet visible from Earth every 76 years. It was last seen in 1986 and will next appear in 2061. This periodic appearance has been documented by astronomers for centuries.

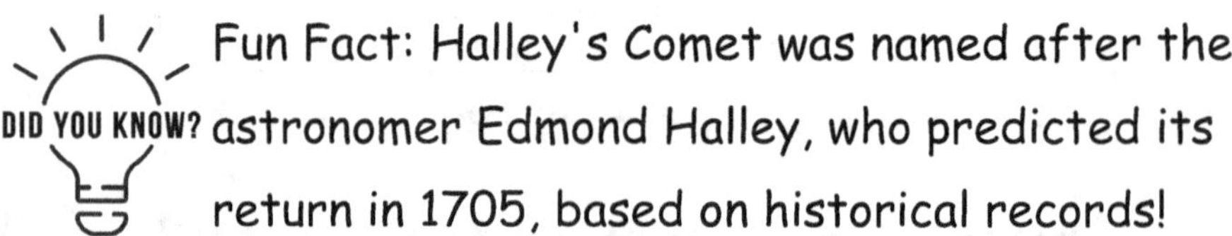

Fun Fact: Halley's Comet was named after the astronomer Edmond Halley, who predicted its return in 1705, based on historical records!

Exoplanets: Distant Oceans to Embrace

Quiz Question

1. What is an exoplanet?

Options

A. A moon of Jupiter
B. An asteroid in the asteroid belt
C. A planet outside our solar system
D. A dwarf planet in the Kuiper Belt

C. A planet outside our solar system

An exoplanet is a planet that orbits a star outside our solar system. These distant worlds vary widely in size, composition, and potential for hosting life. Discovering exoplanets helps scientists understand the diversity of planetary systems in the universe.

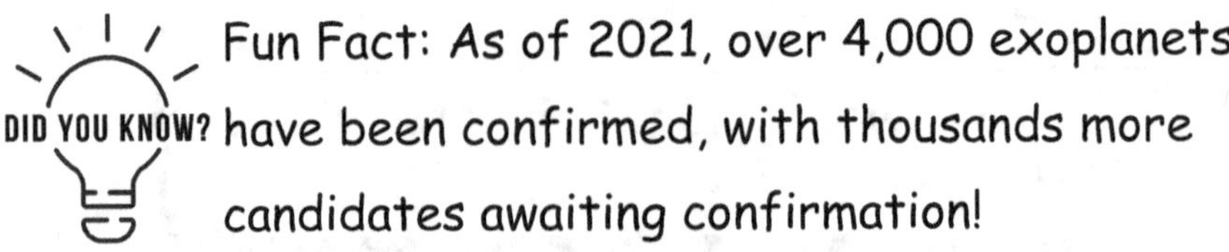

Fun Fact: As of 2021, over 4,000 exoplanets have been confirmed, with thousands more candidates awaiting confirmation!

2. Why is the discovery of water on exoplanets exciting for scientists?

Options

| A. It makes them glow |
| B. It indicates potential for life |
| C. It makes them larger |
| D. It increases their temperature |

B. It indicates potential for life

The discovery of water on exoplanets is exciting because water is essential for life as we know it. Finding water increases the chances that these distant worlds could support life, making them prime targets for further study.

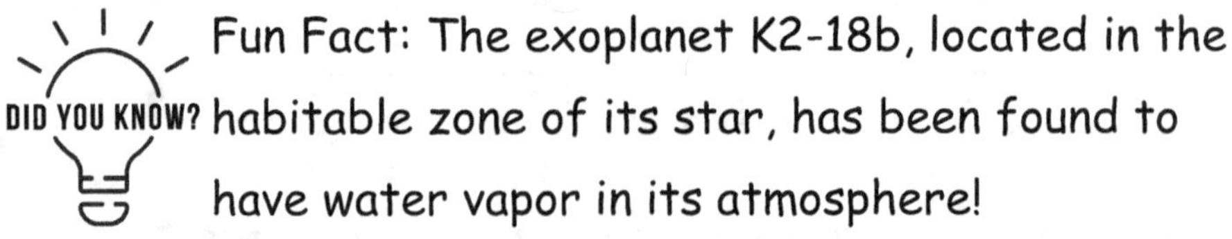

Fun Fact: The exoplanet K2-18b, located in the habitable zone of its star, has been found to have water vapor in its atmosphere!

Exoplanets: Distant Oceans to Embrace

Quiz Question

3. How do scientists detect water on exoplanets?

Options

A. By landing spacecraft on them

B. By analyzing light spectra

C. By listening for sounds

D. By measuring temperatures

B. By analyzing light spectra

Scientists detect water on exoplanets by analyzing the light spectra emitted or absorbed by the planet's atmosphere. Specific wavelengths of light indicate the presence of water vapor, ice, or liquid water.

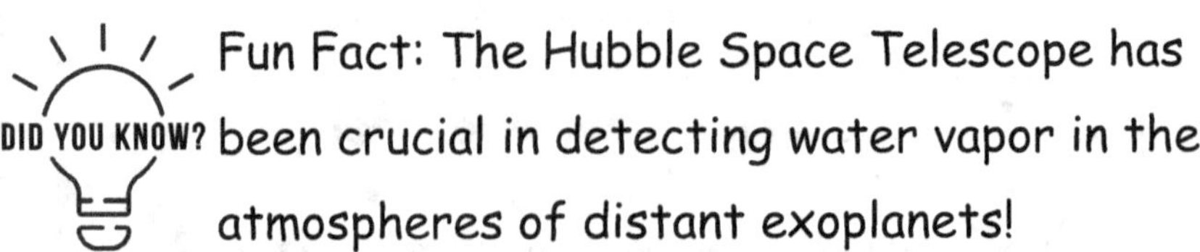

Fun Fact: The Hubble Space Telescope has been crucial in detecting water vapor in the atmospheres of distant exoplanets!

Exoplanets: Distant Oceans to Embrace

4. What is the 'habitable zone' around a star?

A. The region with the most asteroids

B. The area with the highest temperatures

C. The distance where liquid water can exist

D. The region with the brightest light

C. The distance where liquid water can exist

The 'habitable zone' around a star is the range of distances where conditions are just right for liquid water to exist on a planet's surface. This zone is often referred to as the "Goldilocks Zone" because it's not too hot and not too cold.

• • • • • • • • • • • • • • • • • • • •

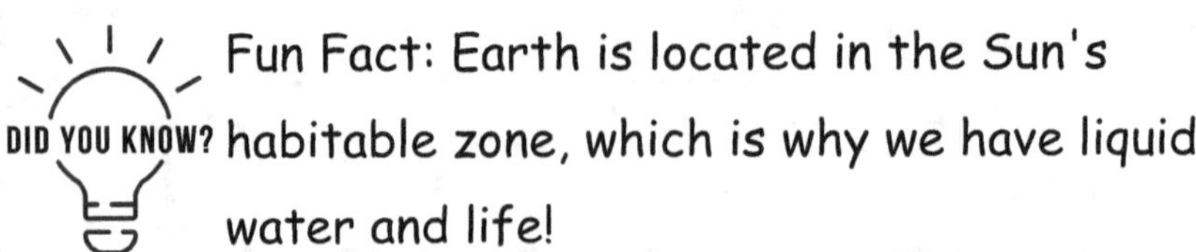

Fun Fact: Earth is located in the Sun's habitable zone, which is why we have liquid water and life!

Quiz Question

5. What makes ocean worlds like Europa and Enceladus exciting for exploration?

Options

A. Their size

B. Their rocky surfaces

C. Their subsurface oceans

D. Their high temperatures

C. Their subsurface oceans

Ocean worlds like Europa (a moon of Jupiter) and Enceladus (a moon of Saturn) are exciting because they have subsurface oceans beneath their icy crusts. These hidden oceans could potentially harbor life, making them intriguing targets for future exploration missions.

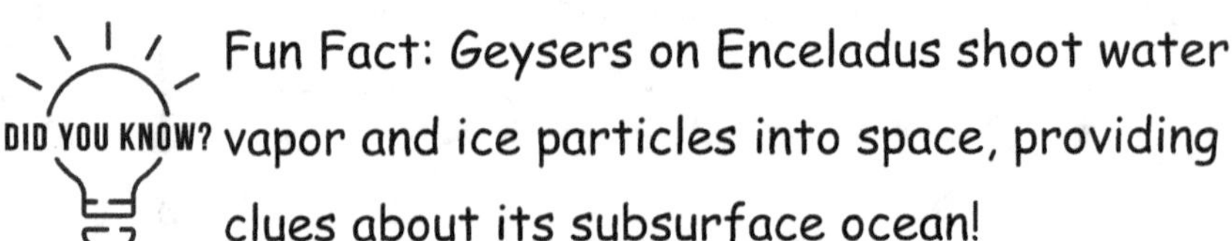

Fun Fact: Geysers on Enceladus shoot water vapor and ice particles into space, providing clues about its subsurface ocean!